EARLE LABOR, MANAGING EDITOR

THE CEA CRITIC

CENTENARY COLLEGE
SHREVEPORT, LA. 71104

THE ART OF
ERNEST HEMINGWAY

THE ART OF

ERNEST HEMINGWAY

HIS WORK AND PERSONALITY

JOHN ATKINS

SPRING BOOKS · LONDON

Published by
Spring Books
Westbook House • Fulham Broadway • London
This edition first published 1964
Second impression 1965

Copyright 1952 by John Atkins
Printed in Czechoslovakia
by Tisk, Brno
T 1456

CONTENTS

Chapter   *Page*

  Preface   vii

  I Natural Man   1

  II Political Man   21

 III Mirror of Society   46

 IV That Famous Style   61

  V The Champion   94

 VI War   116

 VII The Mechanics of Fear 135

VIII The Life of Despair   146

 IX Myth-Making   166

  X Culture and Tradition 178

 XI Feeling and Sensibility 192

 XII A Glimpse of Beauty 204

XIII Morality: or Feeling Good 207

XIV Love and Sex   217

 XV The Women   234

XVI The Old Man and the Sea 244

XVII Coda   248

Appendix A: Bibliography 251

Appendix B: Hemingway on the English 253

ACKNOWLEDGMENTS

In writing this book I have been very fortunate in the assistance I have received from friends in America, from where so much of my material had to come. No one could have worked harder on my behalf than Dr. Bernard Raymund. It is not easy selecting others by name but I feel I should mention Malcolm Cowley for his advice and Frank Steinecke and Charyce Bergeron for their assistance. I must also place on record Mr. Hemingway's own helpfulness.

1952   J. A.

Frontispiece by Karsh (Camera Press Ltd.)

PREFACE

When I heard the news of Hemingway's death on the wireless someone asked me if it was suicide. (Having written a book on him I naturally knew.) Almost indignantly I replied that it couldn't be. It was impossible that one who had lived his life so wholeheartedly should throw it away. Later, after I had had time to think, it seemed just as incredible that someone who knew how to handle firearms should shoot himself accidentally. Some of his obituarists made play with the Freudian notion of a death-wish. Such ideas are often discussed in rather cavalier fashion. Hemingway was fascinated by violence and death. Is it therefore true to say that he was acting out his death-wish? Rather glib, one might think – especially as another school of amateur psychologists see in the very same characteristics the marks of a therapy by which Hemingway was painfully working his way back to complete inner health. Unmotivated accident is still a possibility, and the view that Hemingway was suffering from hypertension brought on by high blood pressure, which caused him to handle his guns too confidently and carelessly, must also be considered. Colonel Cantwell in *Across the River* suffered in the same way. But then Hemingway's own father committed suicide. Such acts are not hereditary in the literal sense, but can they be imitative? Or can heredity cause like reactions to like sets of circumstances? The question remains open.

The first edition of this book was written while Hemingway was still alive. He had just published *The Old Man,* but during the remaining period of his life, nearly ten years, he did not bring out another book. All he could show for these years was a few articles in *Life* and *Look,* a pathetic output for one who might be expected to be at the height of his literary powers. (He was 61, an age when many writers are at their best.) At the time I wrote I had no indication that Hemingway might have been written out. The reports on what he did write but did not publish during those years are very confusing – not even his widow seems to be certain. At one time we were told of a huge military epic, a modern *War and Peace,* with its action on land and sea and in the air; but recently we have heard less of this and instead have been told of something much less ambitious – and significantly, much less creative: a retrospective account of his formative early years in Steinian Paris.[1] But the presumption that Hemingway had lost his creative power is a stong one. There can be no worse fate for a writer, and we would do well to bear it in mind when thinking of his end. This could support the idea of suicide, but it does not require the mechanics of the death-wish.[2]

At the time I wrote there was only one other

[1] There was also *The Dangerous Summer,* parts of which appeared in *Life.* Said to be 120,000 words long, it was promised in book form for 1961, but no more has been heard of it.

[2] During his last year Hemingway suffered from ill-health, a new experience for him. Combined with creative failure, this might have been sufficient to induce a suicidal mood.

critical work on Hemingway, the symposium edited by John K. M. McCaffery. Most of the reviewers at the time did not seem to know Hemingway's work personally (except through the medium of a dying memory), and they preferred to quote Wyndham Lewis's stupid and insensitive essay, which led them to a disparagement of the books. In protest I did not mention this essay, as it seemed better to ignore it than to draw the attention of still more people to it by frontal attack. But shortly after my own book appeared there came an extremely interesting study by Philip Young. I understand that Hemingway tried to prevent the publication of this book. Its treatment was very intimate, far more intimate than my own, and if its diagnosis was accurate it was a brilliant piece of work. If, on the other hand, the diagnosis was specious and only apparently consistent, it was a piece of impudence. According to Hemingway, it was a collection of mistaken conclusions based upon partial information, and it gave a falsely psychopathic notion of his processes.

It seems to me that Young's book is genuinely valuable for its delineation of Hemingway's fear, particularly in its early stages as found in Nick Adams. Most of us agree that Hemingway spent a large part of his life fighting his fear, which is an honourable thing to do, and a very different thing from supporting a death-wish. Many of us had been puzzled by our own reactions to those early stories – on the surface they seemed pointless and yet we felt they contained some deep significance. It is to Young's credit, I think, that he revealed this significance by showing the subject matter to be the aftermath of fear – and it was Hemingway's fear, which we all knew existed. One drawback to this view is that it makes Hemingway out to be a more automatic writer than is usually supposed, but this is the tendency of all modern criticism. We do not like to think that any writer can do anything but write about himself, which is why some critics cannot forgive Shakespeare for passing on so little personal information to posterity.

Dr. Hemingway, the author's father, killed himself in 1928. Young shows that it is implied that Nick Adams' father did the same. So did Robert Jordan's father in *For Whom the Bell Tolls*. Were all these men cowards, who finally could not conquer their fears? And if they were, was Hemingway also one? It is not a point on which we should pronounce too glibly because if we decide that Hemingway did kill himself, and for that reason, a very large part of modern psychological theory seems to fall to the ground. If ever a man should have been able to 'write out' his fear, it was Hemingway. It is assumed today that art is, among other things, a healing process. If, despite all his efforts, Hemingway failed to heal his psychic wounds, what can be left to recommend the method? All his life he had exposed himself (over-exposed himself, claims Young) to the things he feared. It may be a distasteful thing to discover, but I cannot help feeling that Young virtually foretold self-destruction.

Looking back, I feel that the key to Hemingway is probably to be found in *Death in the Afternoon*, if we

wish to pin it down to one book. A mysterious publication called *The Dangerous Summer*, which partially
appeared in *Life* in 1961 and has not since been heard
of, involved a return to the two subjects of the earlier
book, Spain and bullfighting. In 1932 his hero was
Maera the bullfighter, who never gave up fighting
the probability of a violent death. His favourite
picture seemed to be 'the fighter's face drawn with
the strain of maintaining a bravery that is not there.'
His search was for the wound that might restore the
courage taken away by an earlier wound – but how
many wounds did a man need? Did not those
Spanish and Second World War adventures suffice?
Or the plane accidents?[1]

The *aficionado* develops the sense of tragedy and,
with it, ritual. The minor aspects of the sport or
game are not important. The death of the bull, the
victory of the fighter, they are what matter. And
somewhere here lurks the totalitarian excuse, the
infection that took possession of Hemingway for a
brief period, the notion that any crime may be
excused by the nobility of the greater process. I
think Hemingway briefly (though never enthusiasti-
cally) accepted such arguments because the peculiar
demands of bullfighting prepared his mind for such

[1] In 1954 Hemingway's obituaries were written because
his plane crashed in Uganda, and the first people to see
it from the air saw no signs of life. He had a wrenched
arm, transferred to another plane, which looped on take-
off and crashed in flames. This time he suffered a ruptured
kidney and liver, a collapsed intestine and a fractured
skull. Incidentally, the skull had been fractured previously
in a motor accident.

dishonesty. He dispensed with the 'glory words', as he called them, but became more attracted by the 'glory ideas'. It did not last, but he found a refuge in ritual that the bleakness of Anglo-Saxon life could not offer. He wanted to meet death and its servant, violence, honestly and cleanly, but not fearlessly, because the very idea of doing it without fear was a romantic invention. Yet apart from a few experiments he could not face danger personally in the bullring, nor could he really encounter it while hunting Big Game. Big Game sounds dangerous, and Macomber could manage to lose his life in pursuit of it (it was the deadly Wife who got him), but a man as honest as Hemingway could not really pretend that he was doing anything more than face death vicariously in the course of these two activities.[1] It must surely be true that more lives have been lost in American football that on African safari, yet Hemingway insisted that man versus animal is a contest with death, while team games are artificial dramas of victory and defeat. In fact, most of the time the death and violence are merely observed, the victims are other people and other animals.

But we cannot dismiss *Death in the Afternoon* just because it does not satisfy a theory, whether it is the author's or the critics'. It is a very serious book.

[1] Of course I do not wish to disparage Hemingway's courage. In Spain in 1953 he says he went into a wolf's cage to play with the wolf. The wolf couldn't much more than bite him, and the chances were against hydrophobia. They got on well together.

Green Hills of Africa was a later attempt to repeat the formula, but the seriousness had become a mannerism. In the bullring he had found the death of the bull to be tragic, whereas that of the horse was merely comic. For a while this idea took hold of his mind fairly strongly, and there was a temptation to regard all innocent victims, whether in war or sport, politics or gangsterism, as comic. If the extended modern use of the word 'comic' gives a false idea of Hemingway's feeling in the matter, we could replace it by 'unimportant'. The feeling didn't last, yet much of the quality of *Death in the Afternoon* comes from this false premise, just as the genuine greatness of a Napoleon comes out of a vicious lust for power. For the premise is false: the bull is no less innocent than the horse, and only man (and a particular kind of Latin at that) would have him so. Who was comic in *The Old Man* – Santiago or the Fish? And was *For Whom the Bell Tolls* a gallant failure because all the comedians are, for once in Hemingway's career, trying to be tragedians? One recalls his celebrated and partly true statement, 'all bad writers are in love with the epic'. Was Hemingway's tragic a flirtation with this dangerous epic?

But it would be unwise to attempt identification on a big scale between Hemingway and his fictional creations. Young's view that the Harry of 'The Snows of Kilimanjaro' was Hemingway himself is much too simplified. There is something of the author in every one of every author's characters, but complete identification is only found when the invention has shrunk to nothing or monomania has taken possession. The other insight of value (the first is the true significance of the Nick Adams stories) in Young's criticism is his discovery of the 'code hero' — the character who accompanies the actual hero in so many of the stories and provides a standard of 'right' conduct. He is usually a criminal, a sinner or some other occupant of the underworld, but he always sticks to his code, no matter how far he departs from the normal bourgeois code in other matters. (He doesn't squeal, he bears pain stoically.) And the bullfighter is the code hero *par excellence*.

As a writer, that is, one who used words for expression, Hemingway was exceptionally honest. 'The great thing is to last and get your work done and see and hear and learn and understand; and write when there is something that you know; and not before; and not too dammed much after,'[1] he writes in the last paragraph of *Death in the Afternoon*. He hated all falsity, but it was easier to express the distaste with reference to bullfighting. He hated falsity in writing, but it is not easy for someone who doesn't write to see this so clearly. Insincerity can *creep* into writing, unknown to the author, who must be eternally vigilant. Trying too hard to avoid insincerity can produce the greatest insincerity of all. But watching bullfighters, it is easy to spot it. When he was in Spain in 1959 with his friend Bill Davis,

[1] Was this phrase about not writing 'too damned much after' a casual one, or is it something he believed in and followed? Hemingway rarely wrote casually. When we consider the empty years that followed *The Old Man*, it would be well to keep this injunction in mind.

Hemingway followed Antonio Ordonez round the country because he was one of the few who still fought in the classic and honest way. He felt nothing but scorn for those fighters who gave the crowd exactly what they wanted, including 'the telephone', when they leant with one elbow on the exhausted bull's forehead and 'telephoned' their girl friends. And so with the writer. He may accept a commission, but his great sin is to write consciously for a public.

There has been one other book of great value for the Hemingway reader, and that is *The Apprenticeship of Ernest Hemingway: the Early Years*, by Charles A. Fenton. As the title implies, this is biography, not speculation. It takes us up to the publication of the first book of stories, *In Our Time*, in 1924. The importance of Hemingway's early journalistic training in the moulding of his style, especially on the Kansas City *Star*, becomes clear. The *Star* issued a style sheet to its reporters, and the assistant city editor, Pete Wellington, was generally regarded as its guardian. Rule 21 is only one example of the kind of advice that the young Hemingway accepted so seriously and with such lasting effect: 'Avoid the use of adjectives, especially such extravagant ones as *splendid, gorgeous, grand, magnificent*, etc.' Many years later he told an interviewer that he had been 'enormously excited under Pete Wellington's guidance to learn that the English language yields to simplicity through brevity.' On the whole, journalism has been a much more fruitful training ground of literary talent in modern America that in modern England. In England serious writing has come increasingly under the influence of the often profuse and unrestrained don, many of whom would have benefited from the kind of discipline undergone by men such as Hemingway and Thurber on provincial papers. This is not to say that literary honesty came overnight to Hemingway. In 1923 he was capable of writing the following for the Toronto *Star*: 'Anyone who has seen in real life the weak, petulant face of any one of a dozen movie stars who look beautiful on the screen...' It is very doubtful if Hemingway had ever seen a movie star at that time. This is a relapse into the easy kind of superior writing by which an unknown can take it out of someone who is richer or more famous than himself, without any basis in observation. It is a tribute to Hemingway that when we get it from him we notice the insincerity.

One thing that is well brought out by Fenton is Hemingway's immediate and complete distaste for Fascism, even in the earliest days of 1922, when most of the other newspaper correspondents were praising it – the familiar sin of excusing all kinds of rottenness for the sake of a little efficiency here and there. In the Introduction to his selection of war stories, *Men at War*, Hemingway said it was necessary to defeat Fascism at all costs. Even the worst kind of bruiser was writing this sort of thing at the time, many of them with their tongues stuck pretty forcibly into their cheeks. But not Hemingway. His record at least was clean. In the same piece of writing he reiterated his belief that honesty is the first of all literary virtues. One gets tired of reading the same good news, however splendid it may be, but it remains a rather dreary fact that the bases of good work do not change. A writer, wrote Hemingway, 'is either honest or not, as a woman is either chaste or not, and after one piece of dishonest writing he is never the same again.' Well, none of us is perfect, and Hemingway had been guilty of dishonesty in the past (see previous paragraph), but his standards stayed high. Unfortunately, he was beginning to protest too loudly at about this time (1942) – perhaps it was the effect of all that *Esquire* journalism, although the general level of this was not as low as some of the critics liked to pretend. If a writer lies in public, he said, he will be found out, even though the critics, who are in the same conspiracy, will cover up for him during his life time. After that he will not be trusted again, and no one will want to read him. But this is astonishingly naive: a large portion of the human race demand lies as a framework for their lives. They live on deception.

It seems probable that Hemingway did more to set the tone for writing about war than any other modern writer, with the possible exception of Stephen Crane, to whom he himself was greatly indebted. It is astonishing how feeble some of the stories and extracts in his war selection were. There was too much Old Hickory, Uncle Ebenezer Victor, Hugo nonsense about the collection, which might profitably have been cut by half. It highlights the strange paradox in Hemingway, which became clearer as he grew older and his style deteriorated – the sentimentality gnawing away at his toughness. One wonders, while reading, where were the high standards Hemingway set himself. He managed to stave off the worst until the completion of *The Old Man*, at least. But the writing in *The Dangerous Summer* was frequently slack. There were good bullfight descriptions but the whole thing takes place in a frame of childishness – international, fast-set childishness and the kind of childishness that fills the vacuum caused by not knowing what to do half the time.

Some people have dismissed Hemingway as hard-boiled. This is clearly a very hasty judgment, but it is pleasant to find him (recorded by Fenton) telling Maxwell Perkins that he had 'not been at all hard-boiled since July 8th, 1918 – on the night of which I discovered that that also was vanity'. It was the night he was wounded, and 'vanity' is a *mot juste* of ever there was one. It is fascinating to watch the maturity increasing in his Toronto *Star* dispatches from Europe. This work was more important than I had at first imagined: the dedication and the self-imposed discipline are wonderfully (Pete Wellington permitting) impressive. There were, it is true, sloppy and prejudiced passages, but they mostly occurred when he was getting tired of journalism and wanted to tackle something more exacting. We see the famous style maturing: you take a word, you hammer it, you try it out in every possible stance, you exhaust it but first you get everything you can out of it – it's all very much like a description of Dylan Thomas' poetic method that used to be widely quoted during the war years, only he was talking of images, not individual words.

Young suggests that Hemingway, like Lt. Henry

in *Farewell to Arms*, opted out – the one from America, the other from the war. This is not acceptable, and if the other judgments in his book are equally mis-informed we can understand the irritation of Hem-ingway and his widow. For Henry it was escape or death: there was no question of a valid option. Far too much is made of Hemingway's withdrawal from polite society. He was in some ways very well integrated with the established order – he told me in a letter that he preferred the company of men such as Lord Tedder, the R.A.F. boss, to that of men such as Malcolm Cowley, the critic. It is impossible for a European to think of Hemingway as anything but an American: his vigour, his opinions, his way of expressing them, they are all American.[1] His European and African journeys were necessary to his development but they were no more significant or symbolic of expatriation than the journeys of thousands of others wealthy enough to buy whatever experiences they consider fruitful or productive or therapeutic. It was D. H. Lawrence who opted out, not Hemingway. Henry James forsook America, not Hemingway. He had a hearty contempt for the kind of society to be found in New York, but not too much should be read into this. It's equivalent to turning away from commercialism or bourgeois ethics — but every man turns away from something.

Hemingway did spend the greater part of his life outside the United States, but this exile did not

---

[1] In the first paragraph of *The Dangerous Summer* (*Life*, 1960) he calls Spain 'the country that I loved more than any other except my own.'

express the essence of his feeling. He chose the exile because he was looking for a particular kind of experience; he did not choose the experience because he was pathologically obsessed with exile in the form of anti-Americanism. He could be extremely caustic in his references to certain aspects of American life, but this never became the centre of his literary existence. It is significant that this type of criticism does not appear in his major work. He preferred to praise Spanish bullfighters than to castigate American politicians. He was one of the most positive writers there has ever been. Once, comparing the Italian and American temperaments, he referred to the humiliation felt by the Italians after the Caporetto defeat, and added that in similar circumstances the Americans would have produced a vaudeville quartet calling themselves The Caporetto Kids. This is fun, even bitter fun, but it is not searing, heartfelt, burning Laurentian belly-socking.

The crazy season for Hemingway criticism is yet to come. Before I finish, I would like to offer some critic of the future this fascinating association: all those bulls in the afternoon and the Chicago stockyards, in whose shadow the young Hemingway grew up. It's the Yankee bullfight — without the horse!

CHAPTER I

NATURAL MAN

I MIGHT as well be frank and admit that although there are many things I wish to say about Ernest Hemingway and more especially his work, I am rather puzzled about where to start. Somehow one has to find his centre of gravity, the point at which all forces remarkably create a state of rest. It is something like the job the American statisticians gave themselves when they set out to find the population centre of the United States. But that is an exact science. The study of Hemingway is not. At about the time when Hemingway's influence was at its highest a band of literary critics attempted to prove that literary values could be ascertained like the speed of light. It was fitting that Hemingway should look over their shoulders as a reproving monument of unreliability, and it is interesting to note that the speed of light changes as men's measuring rods become more efficient. Hemingway is an excellent shot and a champion fisherman but you never know from one year to the next how he's going to write. Following his work through years is like travelling rough country.

But I don't want to stress this irregularity. That would be a pointless thing to do – one has only to think of a few writers now referred to as 'classics', writers like Shelley and Thackeray, and even Wells, to realise that creative writing follows no smooth path. And the interesting writers do progress, though not always so radically as Milton who began his career as an orthodox Christian and finished it doubting the divinity of Christ. But today the terms are different and the way is different, and it is the vast difference that appealed to Hemingway's admirers. Apart from a half-superstitious respect for religion he has shown none of the concern for it that has been so characteristic of those who preceded him and those who followed him. A large number of articles and a very few books have drawn our attention to the matters that have agitated the mind and sensibility of Ernest Hemingway: war, violence, The Lost Generation, war, exile, frustration, death and war. One critic has noticed the pattern of myth and ritual in both life and work. My own contribution will be a study of the central part played by the diagnosis of fear, chiefly in his early work. But a very important aspect of his development, and one we cannot afford to neglect, is his shift from the portrayal of Natural Man to that of Political Man, and back again.

I borrow these terms from Edwin Muir.[1] For many years Hemingway had been the literary personification of Natural Man. All kinds of widely differing people looked to him as the writer who best expressed their own longings. The only thing they had in common was a dislike of restraint, though frequently only in one field, remaining perfectly conventional in others. Young men who enjoyed the idea of free love and constant drinking could find their type-heroes in Hemingway. Other men who believed the real test of manhood was a refusal to be

[1] 'Natural Man and Political Man', *New Writing*.

squeamish found that attitude plainly expressed by Hemingway. Hemingway managed to amalgamate the attitudes of people who in other ways were congenitally antagonistic. It is another way of saying that Hemingway is the best modern example of a writer who pleases the critics and entertains the general reading public. Of course, they like him for different reasons. The general reader enjoys what he says and the critic is entranced by the way he says it. But it also happened that the luck was with Hemingway. He came to maturity at one of those times when philistinism and sophistication shook hands. There have always been many people who assume with great simplicity that the life of man is nasty, brutish and short and think it best that way. Now and again we get a philosopher like Hobbes who agrees, probably reluctantly, and today, with the advent of fashionable barbarism, we have critics who also appear to welcome this point of view.

A lot of spadework had been performed to make Hemingway possible. Wagner, Darwin and Freud had accustomed people to the idea of the animal under the skin. Lawrence flayed it and paraded it. A large public was ready for the defeat of Galsworthy who had in fact done his bit by revealing the shams of society. The European tradition was one of conflict between reason and impulse. Dante, Shakespeare, Balzac and Tolstoy had all written from the same foundations, of man suspended between good and evil. But modern man has put aside this conception of conflict and has replaced it by one of development. We are neither good nor evil, we are entirely neutral in our original values. We can envisage a better state, but rather for men than for Man. We are tired of abstractions. Dante's Man existed in relation to the nine heavens and the Heaven of the Fixed Stars, and the fight was for his soul. But the teeming men of our world exist in relation chiefly to each other and they take an overriding interest in their bellies or, when they are full, other people's bellies. The vision is political and sociological. The concern is not with present virtue but with future welfare, which can be controlled. Control is exercised not through prayer and invocation but through machinery and administration. What men need today is more *things* — more food, more houses, more clothes, more entertainment. We must remember that while the more responsible members of society may express their aims in this way, there are others who know, with varying degrees of candour, that what they really want is more money, more women, more drinks and more drugs. But men's needs are also the best channels through which they can be conditioned. If men need food more than anything else, the first man to give them food will be their accepted master. And so we have new popes and new priests and we also have the friars to spread the new doctrine and assist in adjustment to changing ideas. The world was ready for a writer who could give primacy to *things*. Some people felt that Europe was sinking under a surfeit of unrealised ideas. For every Hemingway there were a dozen Spenglers.

A traditional European, product of a traditional education, saw a descent into barbarism. He wasn't sure about the true nature of what was happening in Russia, he was less doubtful about Italy, and in the case of Germany he said chaos is come again. Denis Saurat in *Modernes* reminded his readers that the 17th century had exalted reason, the 19th century romantics had enthroned emotion, but it was in the 20th century that this trend tipped into a search for sensation. Our civilised onlooker hears his values being ridiculed, was informed that the very thing he had been taught to distrust, his animal nature, was his only admirable possession. What the senses demanded, they should be given. An old nursery song which acquired adult currency put it, Give a dog a bone. Later it was realised that acquisition could be increased enormously if it were properly organised. The animals trooped into politics.

Perhaps most men in all periods have been more concerned with things than with ideals or abstract values. It is a condition of most lives. But Hemingway wrote of men who were not tied to things yet concentrated on them of their own free will. Men such as Francis Macomber, for instance (a late example). He was one of the privileged animals. Mind to him was a secondary product, designed to increase efficiency in the enjoyment of sensation. He knew his wife did not love him, was wealthy and would never leave him.

> He knew about that, about motor cycles – that was earliest – about motor cars, about duck-shooting, about fishing, trout, salmon and big-sea, about sex in books, many books, too many books, about all court games, about dogs, not much about horses, about hanging on

to his money, about most of the other things his world
dealt in, and about his wife not leaving him.[1]

Note the books, not part of a liberal educations, as it
used to be called, but an avenue to sex. By his concentration on the material aspect of life, through
the medium of the catalogue, Hemingway evokes
thought and feeling. We know that we are not concerned with the thinking animal, which is a defini-
tion of man, but with an appetite. Of course, we
exaggerate the significance of our terms. These new
animals were often highly intelligent. But their intelligence was bent to the service of the beast. Macomber's life was reasonably respectable, if not absolutely
harmonious, because his wife had money. Minority
pleasures are sometimes considered vicious but never
low.

War, or more exactly battle, gave Hemingway his
real chance to exhibit a world which consisted entirely
of things. Millions of things, most of them broken,
most of them useless, and filling the spectator with
a sense of despair and desolation – but the despair
was the man's, not the thing's. Nick Adams saw
what was left when the tide of battle had rolled on –

> a field kitchen, it must have come over when things
> were going well; many of the calf-skin-covered haver-
> sacks, stick bombs, helmets, rifles, sometimes one
> butt-up, the bayonets stuck in the dirt, they had dug
> quite a little at the last; stick bombs, helmets, entrench-
> ing tools, ammunition boxes, starshell pistols, their
> shells scattered about, medical kits, gas masks,

[1] 'The Short Happy Life of Francis Macomber.'

6

and so on, an inventory of defeat. There is no comment. Nick passes on. Hemingway is silent. We may sigh if we wish. But the important thing to notice is that we see what a rabbit sees, only our elevation is greater. We can name the items. An older generation would have said it didn't bear thinking of. Nick and the rabbit see no reason why we should think of these things.[1]

It might be said that there is a difference between war and secular killing, if I may use the term. We have adopted an attitude of acceptance towards the inevitability of war. War is always essential usually to prevent ourselves being enslaved or killed. There is no viciousness in the killing. (This is the kind of social sanction we create to excuse a highly dubious business.) After all, even Tolstoy had reported the battle of Sebastopol with an entirely modern coolness, and Tolstoy had a large-size conscience. But secular killing, now that is a different matter, it is a bad case of malice prepense, and we are justified in shuddering. And so when Edwin Muir wishes to illustrate Hemingway's naturalism he chooses not one of the war stories but 'The Killers'[2]. He points out that the two gunmen are mechanical murderers and the victim a mechanical murderee: 'they are all equally conditioned; and there is nothing to be said about them, except that they evoke the kind of pity one might feel in watching some hunting beast pulling down and killing its prey'[3]. Then Mr. Muir notices a discrepancy in his terminology; he has

[1] 'A Way You'll Never Be', *Winner Take Nothing*.
[2] From *Men Without Women*.   [3] Edwin Muir, *ibid*.

7

stressed Hemingway's naturalism yet the characters
he cites are automata. But the fault is with the men
rather than with Mr. Muir. When an attempt is
made to eliminate thought and emotion and live on
sensation alone, the result is not a beautiful, strong
beast. It is simply a woefully circumscribed man. 'In
his short story Mr. Hemingway is sure of only one
thing, the immediate sensation, and being a scrup-
ulously honest writer, he confines himself to that and
leaves out thought and emotion as much as possible.'[1] This limitation of the man to an extent where
his humanity itself is impaired drew forth a rebuke
from Aldous Huxley which Hemingway thought
worth while answering. But I will come to that later.

The Hemingway myth has become so strong it
has strayed a long way from the reality, as myths always do. For instance, it is an article of faith among
critics who read the early novels as young men and
have never returned to them though they frequently
refer to them in articles on 'The Modern Novel', that
Hemingway never comments on his material. This is
untrue, and I shall deal with it in greater detail in
another chapter. Hemingway is not only aware that
the people he writes of and frequently admires
possess automatic processes. He even stops to tell us
in case we have missed it. For instance, of a bullfighter he says:

> He thought in bull-fight terms. Sometimes he had a
> thought and the particular piece of slang would not
> come into his mind and he could not realise the
> thought. His instincts and his knowledge worked auto-

[1] Edwin Muir, *ibid.*

matically, and his brain worked slowly and in words. He knew all about bulls. He did not have to think about them. He just did the right thing. His eyes noted things and his body performed the necessary measures without thought. If he thought about it, he would be gone.[1]

The slang phrases are like counters in a gambling game. There is also something of the primitive faith in the name of a thing. Name your god and you will have his power on your side.

'Probably no one else has described more vividly,' writes Mr. Muir, 'the horror of the natural man's life when he is driven and goaded and denied natural satisfaction, and retires into himself to lick his wounds or seek forgetfulness in drink or sex'.[2] This is true. It is we, heirs of civilisation, who feel the horror. We don't know whether the killers realise how miserable their lives are. It is certain they don't find their lives sordid for their vocabulary contains no such word. But not all Hemingway's characters are mere tough quys with neural systems scarcely more complicated than an amoeba's. There are the journalists and the wealthy sportsmen who have opted for the natural life, and we see them in its toils when it is too late, and it seems likely that they are people who suffer. The lucky ones are those who have not been trained to sensibility. It could not be pleasant to know that you are making a bad end, deprived of the dignity which used to be Western man's pride – an end like that of the dying man in 'The Snows of Kilimanjaro', probably Hemingway's

[1] 'The Undefeated', *Men Without Women.*   [2] *Ibid.*

favourite story. 'So this was the way it ended in a bickering over a drink.' He was going fast and she knew it yet the animal fight was maintained to the bitter end. The supreme question on his death-bed was: Should he have a whisky-soda?

If there is no trust in life it is too late to institute it during the last five minutes. He and his mate would die as they lived, snapping. At one moment a stray influence from a moralising past invaded his mind. The only thing he had ever liked to do was to hurt her. There was the animal and at the same time the man, watching. He recognised the instinct he had fostered, to kill others that he might live. In these later stories ('Macomber', 'Kilimanjaro') Hemingway has really torn away the bandages of existence. Even more than in *Fiesta,* his first novel, we see the two natures locked in combat. Towards the end the dying man makes use of a familiar modern metaphor. The party's over, he tells himself. Death has come to collect and it's not even a sombre occasion. It just goes on too long. But the old traditions are dead, death is merely the end of something, dying is boring and there are no priests to disguise its triviality. We don't know how a dog dies but it may be like that.

In fact, in the celebrated 'Natural History of the Dead', which first appeared in *Death in the Afternoon,* Hemingway announces that most men die like animals anyway. Some die quickly from a scratch, others linger in the throes of terrible mutilation. This seems reasonable enough. There is no great divide between a dead man and a dead cow. Yet it is not logical to assume that if in death they are alike, so are they in life. At the time of his first war experience Hemingway had not seen a 'natural' death. When he did it was from Spanish influenza, which is too horrible to contemplate. But once again our terms are getting out of hand. The 'natural' man, as a consequence of his life, dies an 'unnatural' death, i.e. from loss of blood. But if natural behaviour results in unbridled acquisitiveness, then violent death will become comparatively normal. It is a reversion of meaning similar to that which has overtaken the word 'public' in 'public school'. It is doubtful if most animals do die violent deaths. The point is that Hemingway appears to think they do. After years of hunting in the woods of Michigan and fishing in its rivers, watching baggage animals being slaughtered by panic-stricken Greeks, and seeing bulls and horses ritually killed in Spain, there is probably justification.

We have always taken it for granted that animals have no souls. That is a human privilege. Death brings darkness, nothingness, except for the elect. Similarly, animal existence is a thing of no significance in a homocentric universe. At the most it is evidence of God's power and variety. When a man forgoes those qualities which are supposed to distinguish him from animals, he shares their supposed oblivion. Lieutenant Henry thinks of the leave he hadn't taken, where everything was cold and fresh and healthful.

> I had gone to no such place but to the smoke of cafés and nights when the room whirled and you needed to look at the wall to make it stop, nights in bed, drunk,

11

> when you knew that that was all there was, and the strange excitement of waking and not knowing who it was with you, and the world all unreal in the dark and so exciting that you must resume again unknowing and not caring in the night, sure that this was all and all and all and not caring.[1]

When you knew that that was all there was... And yet you cannot get rid of the residue of thought, the old nagging habit, which compels you to brood on your condition. It is unlikely that either animals or killers brood. The educated man is trapped in the traces of sensibility.

The midway position in which many modern men are liable to find themselves produces its problems. If the aim is a simplification of life it is not always achieved. One result is the chronic inarticulateness of lovers, greater than at any time in previous literature. The precise loquacity of lovers in, say, Maria Edgeworth or Thackeray, though not entirely unreal (for they practised verbal expression and regarded it as a virtue) is tiresome to modern taste. But the modern man who in many cases replaces the word love by the word sex is at the mercy of forces he has not only ceased to understand but does not wish to understand. A smattering of Freud is no substitute for the literature of love which, unless we have deceived ourselves completely, possesses its own brand of reality. I mean by this that even if love is an invention it is one of the necessary ones like Voltaire's God, and the human race is soaked in its mythos. The ex-lovers in 'The End of Something'[2] scarcely

[1] *Farewell to Arms.*   [2] From *In Our Time.*

dare look at each other because they lack all understanding. Nick gropes for reasons but is utterly
baffled.

> He was afraid to look at Marjorie. Then he looked at
> her. She sat there with her back toward him. He
> looked at her back. It isn't fun any more. Not any
> of it.
>
> She didn't say anything. He went on. I feel as
> though everything was gone to hell inside of me. I
> don't know, Marge. I don't know what to say.

The title is brilliant. The end of Something. Nick
continued to be mystified. He felt an elemental force
had worked through him. Later he discussed the
affair with his friend Bill.

> 'All of a sudden everything was over', Nick said.
> 'I don't know why it was. I couldn't help it. Just like
> when the three-day blows come now and rip all the
> leaves off the trees'.[1]

Sometimes there is allusion or reference to the
intelligence that a human animal may possess. To
Marie in *To Have and Have Not* her husband Harry
Morgan is merely a magnificent animal. She wants
nothing more. When Augustin and Pilar are discussing other members of the partisan band in *For
Whom the Bell Tolls*, Augustin calls the gypsy an
animal. Pilar reminds him that he also is an animal
but with a qualification: he is intelligent. And then
Augustin puts his finger on a point we have already
noticed: animalism pure and simple is not enough.
The intelligence must still plan and direct. 'To make
war all you need is intelligence. But to win you need

[1] 'The Three-Day Blow', from *In Our Time*.

talent and material.' True, he rates intelligence low. But fundamentally it is liable to develop into a chicken-or-egg argument.

If we are to think in terms of purpose (and we can be sure that killers do, even if they have not always developed powers of generalisation), then what is a fit purpose, or perhaps I should say the natural, inevitable purpose, of those of us who are not killers? There can be little doubt about Lieutenant Henry's answer: 'I was not made to think. I was made to eat. My God, yes. Eat and drink and sleep with Catherine'.[1] This is the clearest expression of a natural man's philosophy to be found in Hemingway's work – but again we must be careful of our terminology. To attribute philosophy to a natural man is as fallacious as the attribution of magical doctrines to African natives. The African acts, we interpret. Sociologists interpret killers. Lieutenant Henry, Nick Adams and Jake Barnes are all hybrids, intermittently evaluating their automatic actions. As when Jake realised why the fiesta was his ideal environment. 'Everything became quite unreal finally and it seemed as though nothing could have any consequences. It seemed out of place to think of consequences during the fiesta.'[2] It was Jake's newspaper training that caused him to think about consequences. Romeo the bullfighter would not have done it.

In *Death in the Afternoon* Hemingway explained the importance of *cojones* (testicles) to the bullfighter. Without them he is nothing. It is, of

[1] *Farewell to Arms.*   [2] *Fiesta.*

course, a mystical term. *Cojones* are the seat of virility just as the belly can be the seat of witchcraft. And in this world of unconscious motivation virility is equated with virtue. The lover possessing great stamina is, rather unrealistically, the physical superman. Similarly references are made to Harry Morgan's *cojones*.[1] Harry always satisfies his wife and therefore, it is implied, he is fearless and strong.

In mapping out the topography of the natural man it is simple enough to determine the roots of happiness. It is merely a state of complete disinhibition, without thought and with full exercise for *cojones* in both physical and metaphorical senses. Walking towards the river where he was going to fish 'Nick felt happy. He felt he had left everything behind, the need for thinking, the need to write, other needs. It was all back of him.'[2] This sounds somewhat autobiographical. Writing is hard work for Hemingway. Fishing is pleasure. It is also worth noting that this story shows natural man at his most attractive. The sensations are extraordinarily keen yet not violent. It is a reminder that natural man always existed in even the most sensitive make-up and classical period – Hemingway, Wordsworth and Gray might have walked that road together without hating each other.[3] There is a very potent suggestion here. To be anything but natural in a natural environment is to invite mental as well as physical mal-

[1] *To Have and Have Not.*
[2] 'Big Two-Hearted River: Part I', from *In Our Time.*
[3] In *The Torrents of Spring* Scripps imagines himself 'striding through the Lake Country with Wordsworth'.

adjustment. It is the insistence on natural conduct, in its simplified form, in the big city that causes the trouble. 'Excuse me while I wash. In big city I guess you wash your neck', Hemingway is alleged to have said to Lillian Ross.[1] This was one occasion when he made a concession. For the Hemingway attitudes and those expressed in his books are so much of a piece we are justified in looking upon him as the natural man plus the habit of thought. Like Jake Barnes and Lieutenant Henry. But we must leave the consideration of Hemingway himself till later.

The final reduction of this attitude is made when the elementary thought processes of both man and animal become identical. In the past inferior nature writers used to endow their animals with powers of thought and emotion similar to the author's. Henry Williamson reduced an animal's feelings to the little we know of them: sensation only. Hemingway has gone further and bracketed the man with the animal. Watch Macomber and the lion. The lion

> turned his heavy head and swung away toward the cover of the trees as he heard a cracking crash and felt the slam of a .30-06 220-grain solid bullet that bit his flank and ripped in sudden hot scalding nausea through his stomach. He trotted, heavy, big-footed, swinging wounded full-bellied, through the trees toward the tall grass and cover, and the crash came again to go past him ripping the air apart. Then it crashed again and he felt the blow as it hit his lower ribs and ripped on through, blood sudden hot and

[1] Profile, 'How Do You Like It Now, Gentlemen?' *The New Yorker*, 13 May 1950.

frothy in his mouth, and he galloped toward the high grass where he could crouch and not be seen and make them bring the crashing thing close enough so he could make a rush and get the man that held it. Macomber had not thought how the lion felt as he got out of the car. He only knew his hands were shaking and as he walked away from the car it was almost impossible for him to make his legs move. They were stiff in the thighs, but he could feel the muscles fluttering. He raised the rifle, sighted on the junction of the lion's head and shoulders and pulled the trigger. Nothing happened though he pulled until he thought his fingers would break.[1]

This is a most revealing passage. In the first place, it is excellent writing. If it is possible to transfer sensation, it is done here. Secondly, both man and animal are at roughly the same level of mental evolution. (Technologically the man is more advanced because he has a tool.) The word 'thought' is twice used in relation to the man, but on one occasion merely to deny the activity. On the other he thinks his finger might break, which is barely worthy of the ratiocinative process. Although the word is not used of the animal he comes near to it when he plans a trap for his assailant. The lion is a finer specimen. We feel that Macomber would make a very poor lion and that the lion wouldn't even be interested in making a Macomber. In a situation where acuteness is the measure of value the lion has the edge on the man. The 'sudden hot scalding nausea' is nobly contrasted with the fluttering muscles.

Macomber is a weaker specimen of mankind's

[1] 'The Short Happy Life of Francis Macomber.'

newest phase. He fails to become the man he wishes to be. His courage fails him, he has no *cojones*. Later he tries to rectify the failing but it is too late. Contrast him with the picador we are introduced to in another of the later stories, 'The Capital of the World'. 'He lived in a small, tight, professional world of personal efficiency, nightly alcoholic triumph, and insolence.' He did not set his sights too high. He wanted to conquer in a small world and he succeeded. But Macomber was in a mess. His world was not small and tight enough. It sprawled. It was too late to enter the kind of world he wanted. There was no professional world in which he could establish his personal efficiency. He was too well bred to be insolent. It is doubtful if even the bravest lion's reputation is widespread. Macomber's energies had been dissipated. He cut a poor figure alongside Wilson, the professional game hunter, who knew his field and did not stray outside it.

In a symposium on 'The State of American Writing, 1948'[1] R. P. Blackmur, in deploring the readiness of American writers to dismiss as 'spiritual fellaheen' the mass of middlebrow culture, complains that Hemingway is an unsatisfactory alternative because he reduces the human figure to a 'muscular ... jelly of principles without values.' It is impossible to deny the truth of this accusation, although I do not believe a moral charge is ever valid in literature. I mean by this that Hemingway's work is certainly muscle without values (I would prefer to say traditional civilised values) but that he does not

[1] *Partisan Review*, August 1948.

set out nor should he be expected to set out to provide a satisfactory alternative either to middlebrow
culture or highbrow criticism of it. When a writer
like Ruskin does this very thing there are critics, and
often the very ones who had demanded values, who
set up a howl of indignation. The truth is that no
creative writer should ever listen to critics. They can
help the reader to understand but they never help
the writer to write. In the same symposium Leslie A.
Fiedler calls Hemingway an anti-intellectual, brack-
eting him with Wolfe and Faulkner, and Clement
Greenberg lines him up with the 'Western intellectuals', which is presumably a way of saying that he
isn't an intellectual at all. Elsewhere Edgar Johnson
calls him 'an intellectual who has renounced intellectualism'.[1] Having quarrelled with 'the root-
assumption of bohemian-aesthetic intellectualism',
he has been 'derided as a sort of modern Heidelberg
Man, incapable of understanding the things he de-
spised'. We must be careful to realise, however, that
this view of Hemingway is largely deduced. Hemingway has made very few attacks on intellectualism. He
has for the most part avoided any contact with it. His
attacks are largely the result of unprovoked aggres-
sion by critics who disapprove of his characters and
their way of life.

It is also necessary to remind ourselves that
there is more than violence and *cojones* in Hemingway's work. For a period he partially renounced
naturalism and adopted a political attitude. During

[1] 'Farewell the Separate Peace', from *Ernest Hemingway,
the Man and his Work*, edited by John K. M. McCaffery.

this phase there were signs of pity, an emotion rarely exhibited by killers and lions. Stephen Spender draws attention to the story 'Under the Ridge' about the Spanish War. Two instances of unnecessary cruelty by some army police agents arouse hatred in an Extremadurian, a hatred based on a feeling of pity, even a sense of justice. An American Film Unit is so affected it packs up and leaves. This is new. People are showing feelings about cruelty and madness, instead of merely accepting them. Spender writes, 'man's struggle against his own nature has more significance than his nature itself'.[1] This struggle is objectified in politics. It is time to examine Hemingway's version of Political Man.

[1] 'Books and the War', *Penguin New Writing* No. 5.

CHAPTER II

POLITICAL MAN

'THE basis of Hemingway's early writing is a total renunciation of all social frameworks; the separation of the writer from the common activity of his time; the acceptance of a profound isolation as the basis for the writer's achievement.'[1] Nick Adams, Jake Barnes and Lieutenant Henry all agree in ignoring social organisation. Living as near to a natural life as possible they refuse to concern themselves with political or economic structure. The woods of Michigan present their problems but they are the eternal ones. No political fashion disturbs them. Jake Barnes seeks the bullfight, not the civil commotion which was rapidly becoming the familiar climate of Europe. And Lieutenant Henry fought in a distant war for a reason never divulged; but it is a straight fight, without political entanglement.

If we can give a name to a non-existent political attitude it would have to be anarchism. Now and again Hemingway was compelled to notice matters of political significance because his human animals occasionally came into contact with self-confessed political animals. Nine-tenths of the time you could ignore them but there was always the odd occasion when you would be compelled to take up a position. You then showed that politics was an unreal manceuvring, that the highflown phrases had no true meaning. Once again values were deliberately denied.

[1] Maxwell Geismar, *Writers in Crisis*.

There was no essential difference between democracy and tyranny because what really mattered was the animal conflict imposed by our natures. Men with unsatisfied appetites did not bother themselves with abstractions.

The best expression of a political man in Hemingway's work is to be found in a celebrated passage from his story 'The Gambler, The Nun and the Radio'.[1] A Mexican visiting a wounded friend in hospital remarks that religion is the opium of the people. Frazer says nothing but the statement lies in his mind. It has little to do with religion, a great deal with politics. But to Frazer, who resembles Bentham in seeing no difference in value between poetry and pushpin, it is merely one possible selection from an endless variety. If religion is opium, why not anything else among men's many inventions?

> Music is the opium of the people. Old mount-to-the-head hadn't thought of that. And now economics is the opium of the people; along with patriotism the opium of the people in Italy and Germany. What about sexual intercourse; was that an opium of the people? Of some of the people. Of some of the best people. But drink was a sovereign opium of the people, oh, an excellent opium.

There were a number of others he could think of: radio, gambling, ambition, belief in a new form of government. But there was one supreme opium, a universal opium: bread. He had even told the Mexican that marijuana might well be considered the opium of the people. Nothing like calling a dog

[1] From *Winner Take Nothing*.

22

by its real name. In fact, anything that people enjoyed, anything they wanted or needed, was opium.
Anything that got in the way of their immersion in
political programmes, anything that made them less
susceptible to political leaders. 'What you wanted
was the minimum of government, always less government. Liberty, what we believed in, now the name of
a MacFadden publication.' William Saroyan might
have written that.

Hemingway expressed his distaste for political
entanglement again in *Green Hills of Africa*. (Like
Winner Take Nothing, this volume appeared in the
early 'thirties, just before the first hint that Hemingway was devoting more thought to specific political
problems).

> If you serve time for society, democracy, and the other
> things quite young, and declining any further enlist-
> ment make yourself responsible only to yourself, you
> exchange the pleasant, comforting stench of comrades
> for something you can never feel in any other way than
> by yourself. That something I cannot yet define
> completely but the feeling comes.....

He follows with a commonplace yet finely-written
metaphor of the Gulf Stream which flows unceasing-
ly and is never contaminated by the garbage that is
thrown into it – the stream of life passing by all the
various systems of government and remaining un-
changed. The animal will outlive the politician. In
comradeship you find richness; political affiliation
will bring you loneliness because instead of sharing
the real things of life you share its bodiless ideas.

But as not everyone can choose his milieu it is sometimes necessary for even an animal to come to terms with specifically human activity. It is on these occasions that what is usually called 'animal cunning' comes into play. Even in his first book of stories Hemingway was aware of the man who found himself involved in a political situation. It was necessary to make an adaptation. To stand aside as a spectator was becoming more and more dangerous. The old liberal objectivity was doomed and later provided the theme for Spender's *Trial of a Judge* and Rex Warner's *The Professor*. To oppose the dominant party was equivalent to suicide via the concentration camp. The obvious course for the natural man was to align himself with those in power, concealing his disbeliefs. In a very short story called 'The Revolutionist'[1] Hemingway tells us of a young man travelling through Italy, carrying a square of oilcloth from party headquarters written in indelible pencil and requesting help from the comrades because he had suffered badly under the Whites in Budapest. He was not a perfectly natural man because his major interest was art and he preferred Giotto to Mantegna, but his attitude to his political environment was typical of the necessary subterfuge imposed on the man without politics, the man who couldn't distinguish between one opium and another.

In a later story we see an old man being swallowed by war – war being an extension of politics in our world. He was too old to adjust himself like 'the revolutionist', he could only sit and

[1] From *In Our Time*.

watch the countryside being overrun. While the
soldiers were crossing the bridge he sat at the side of
the road and watched. He told the officer he was
without politics. He had been looking after two goats
and a cat and four pairs of pigeons but they had all
gone. He supposed the cat would be safe because it
could look after itself.

> 'I was taking care of animals', he said dully, but no
> longer to me. 'I was only taking care of animals'.
> There was nothing to do about him. It was Easter
> Sunday and the Fascists were advancing toward the
> Ebro.
> It was a grey overcast day with a low ceiling so
> their planes were not up. That and the fact that cats
> know how to look after themselves was all the good
> luck that old man would ever have.[1]

The first book in which Hemingway showed signs
of a political conscience was *To Have and Have Not*.
The theme is suggested by the title. It is the contrast
between wealth and poverty, to the moral disadvantage of the former. We see an incipient political attitude forming among men who have always avoided
such things in the past. They are beginning to think
through their bellies. So far they have barely moved
beyond instinct but it is on instinct and basic dis-
satisfactions that the great modern political movements are based. Harry Morgan is trying to persuade
Al to help him take some Cuban revolutionaries
back to Cuba. Al, a family man, is digging sewers for
seven and a half dollars a week. Harry says:

[1] 'Old Man at the Bridge'.

'My family is going to eat as long as anybody eats. What they're trying to do is starve you Conchs out of here so they can burn down the shacks and put up apartments and make this a tourist town. That's what I hear. I hear they're buying up lots, and then after the poor people are starved out and gone somewhere else to starve some more they're going to come in and make it into a beauty spot for tourists'.

'You talk like a radical', I said.

'I ain't no radical', he said. 'I'm sore. I been sore a long time'.

The interesting thing about this passage is the way both speakers recoil from the radical attribute. They have never concerned themselves with politics and radical is a political term. Politicians are not of their world. However base a politician may be he works in an intellectualised climate. In the simple ethics of men who may themselves be rogues there is something shady about politics – shady in the wrong way. Natural men have their code, and we will examine it later. Now, when they are mystified by the way things are going wrong – social maladjustment, but they would not use the term – they complain angrily, in fact become radicals without a programme, but they would never accept the label. Perhaps later they will accept a new label, but never one sported by professors and rich tourists.

These men could never become political minded in the conventional pre-World War way. In the article already quoted Edwin Muir says that the modern political goal belongs to a different world from Hemingway's and could not be reached by his methods. *To Have and Have Not* was followed by

For Whom the Bell Tolls. Here we see Hemingway and thousands of previously natural men involved in political conflict. But the fighting, lusting man cannot be reborn by adding a few words to his vocabulary: liberty, fraternity and equality. The new goals must be discovered through thought and emotion, whereas Hemingway's contribution was merely an appetite for those three values. Although Harry Morgan and Al are both killed we know what they would have become if life did not become easier for them. They would have complained, they might have joined a Fascist movement, they would have demanded liberty and equality, but their early training and aversion from thought and feeling would have made them enemies of both. When later characters in Hemingway's fiction took over from where Harry Morgan left off, Mr. Muir claims that an unfamiliar sentimentality crept in: 'it was as if we saw Caliban looking for a moment through the eyes of Prospero and, without Prospero's rod, swearing to perform Prospero's miracle with his naked fists'.[1]

We must never forget Hemingway's honesty. Although he frequently writes of deluded men he is not in a state of perpetual delusion himself. I put it in this way because I doubt if the man lives who has not made serious and sometimes foolish mistakes in his political thinking. But there is an excellent instance of clear vision in a description of one of the Cuban revolutionaries taken by Harry Morgan. Even Morgan was disgusted by this man's unneces-

[1] Edwin Muir, *ibid.*

sary, avid brutality. One of the other revolutionaries tries to explain his actions in terms of his past.

> 'You see', the boy said, speaking quietly, 'this man Roberto is bad. He is a good revolutionary but a bad man. He kills so much in the time of Machado he gets to like it. He thinks it is funny to kill. He kills in a good cause, of course. The best cause.'[1]

This is a frank admission of Caliban in Prosperos role. It also shows that there is something wrong with much modern criticism. It is to his credit that Hemingway has described this natural-cum-political man so accurately. To go beyond this and attribute a Cuban revolutionary's state of mind to the author, as is implied by Muir and others, is unfair practice. But it is one that most novelists have complained about. Ford Madox Ford used to get very angry about it.

In fact, the ordinary man does not become a politician until he is hurt. Hemingway knows this and I think he is right. But during the 'thirties many well-educated men became politically-minded without being hurt. In many cases this was admirable. Although it has become fashionable to pour scorn on theoretical politicians (i.e. those who still base their action on their ideals, engendered by thought and emotion) it is probably a healthier sign than a complete lack of interest in other people's condition. But it was among these people that Hemingway's reputation began to go sour. Yet there is often great sanity and a high degree of realism in some of the state-

[1] *To Have and Have Not.*

ments of Hemingway's characters, especially those whom we can occasionally identify with the author with some justification. For instance, Robert Jordan in *For Whom the Bell Tolls* is capable of thought — at least, he is a college teacher. He tries to explain the political situation in America to the members of his partisan group in simple terms. He describes the fabian method of taxing large estates out of existence.

> 'But surely the big proprietors and the rich will make a revolution against such taxes. Such taxes appear to me to be revolutionary. They will revolt against the government when they see that they are threatened, exactly as the fascists have done here', Primitivo said.
> 'It is possible'.
> 'Then you will have to fight in your country as we fight here'.
> 'Yes, we will have to fight'.
> 'But there are not many fascists in your country?'
> 'There are many who do not know that they are fascists but will find it out when the time comes'.
> 'But you cannot destroy them until they rebel?'
> 'No,' Robert Jordan said. 'We cannot destroy them. But we can educate the people so that they will fear fascism and recognise it as it appears and combat it'.

Three points of interest. The politically un-educated partisan can see a point quickly enough when it is put to him in concrete terms. The war has quickened his political wits. Secondly, the statement that there are many who do not know they are fascists is true and arises naturally out of Hemingway's appreciation of people and politics. And thirdly, Robert Jordan says the people must be educated.

Neither Jake Barnes nor Lieutenant Henry would have said such a thing. Education was part of the world they tried to escape. If it is objected that Jordan is a college teacher and naturally talks that way the obvious reply is that Hemingway chose him.

Yet it is a slow process, turning ordinary men into politicians. There is also a vast difference between Americans and Europeans. Apart from the British who, being marginal to Europe, have more in common with the Americans politically than with the continental Europeans, the European is less frightened of political terminology than the American. He has been pushed through so many different political systems and so rapidly that he has become familiar with terms that still make the American feel uncomfortable. You therefore often find a European, especially a Latin, using labels without any precise meaning, a condition that Hemingway was quick to notice. In America one might expect the reality before the label, Huey Long before Fascism. There is no doubt that many self-styled European socialists and communists knew less of the meaning of those terms than many an intelligent sixth-form schoolboy. Even during the First World War men were throwing political terms about with a fine disregard for their significance although they probably had a prophetic value. Lieutenant Henry's drivers, for instance, declared they were socialists. Two of them were alleged to be anarchists because they didn't go to church. Being socialist had something to do with coming from Imola.

'Are you all socialists?'
'Everybody'.
'Is it a fine town?'
'Wonderful. You never saw a town like that'.
'How did you get to be socialists?'
'We're all socialists. Everybody is a socialist. We've always been socialists'.
'You come, Tenente. We'll make you a socialist too'.[1]

He could get no more out of them. This was very early and it was also Italy.

The gap between sheer political indifference and political maturity is a wide one and can only be traversed in stages. First of all there is a baffled discontent, a desire for vengeance, but it still remains outside the overt political framework. That was when we saw Harry Morgan and his friend Al. Next we see men whose ignorance is probably just as great but they have taken the step from political detachment to political attachment (nominal socialists). A third stage is illustrated by Harry Morgan when he lies dying and in halting language announces that you can do nothing alone. This is a pointer to something more than political attachment. Political organisation is now required. The best illustration of this is to be found in *For Whom the Bell Tolls* when the partisans, although still disclaiming political affiliation, admit the need for direction and control. And this was exactly the position in which Robert Jordan found himself. He was helping the Republic because he loved Spain and believed that a Fascist victory would make life unbearable for

[1] *Farewell to Arms.*

31

those who believed in the Republic. But he had no politics, i.e., no body of political doctrine, only a momentary desire to help one side in an existing conflict against the other.

> He was under Communist discipline for the duration of the war. Here in Spain the Communists offered the best discipline and the soundest and surest for the prosecution of the war. He accepted their discipline for the duration of the war because, in the conduct of the war, they were the only party whose programme and whose discipline he could respect.

This partially formulated political standpoint could exist in a number of ways, according to the background of the person involved. Anselmo's background was at the opposite extreme to Robert Jordan's: he was a very simple man who, unlike Jordan, had an animal background, but he was a very gentle animal, an animal with religion. In fact, he belonged to an earlier phase in man's development and did not really belong to the category at all. His influences were pre-Hemingway, it was only his poverty that caused his material life to be led in the company of domestic animals, and the roughness he shared with them had been softened by his faith. But now his religion had been obliterated. To a weaker man this might have been a shattering blow, but he had discovered a new consolation, a political one.

> But one thing I have that no man nor any God can take from me and that is that I have worked well for the Republic. I have worked hard for the good that we will all share later. I have worked my best from the first of

the movement and I have done nothing that I am ashamed of.[1]

His politics are as instinctual and trusting as his religion had been.

Political leaders dislike thoughtful followers. Even a truly democratic leader is chary of the species because thought always produces criticism. The modern totalitarian movements have realised that the most pliable supporter is the most ignorant. The freshly initiated man, the man who is still only aware that something is wrong and actually prefers to be told the solution to thinking it out for himself, is excellent material. Sometimes more loosely co-ordinated movements, including those labelled democratic, have seen the great advantage this fact gives to their enemies, and have in turn demanded a closing of their own ranks. It is well known that in war discipline triumphs over criticism. Robert Jordan felt compelled to stifle his qualms, especially those he felt for the people he was endangering and perhaps leading to death, by a similar brand of reasoning. 'Neither you nor this old man is anything', he says to himself. 'You are instruments to do your duty. There are necessary orders that are no fault of yours, and there is a bridge and that bridge can be the point on which the future of the human race can turn. As it can turn on everything that happens in this war. You have only one thing to do and you must do it.'[2] This recognition by Hemingway of an actual wartime situation was later to bring upon

[1] *For Whom the Bell Tolls.*   [2] *Ibid.*

him fierce accusations by critics who assumed that recognition of a situation implied support of a policy.

Whatever the inner complexion of the change, a Hemingway hero was now openly supporting a political movement. Perhaps, as Muir says, he was applying his former aggressiveness to a political situation, so that he was merely making an adaptation without undergoing any fundamental moral change. Yet, as Stephen Spender pointed out, there is an enormous difference between *Fiesta* and *For Whom the Bell Tolls*[1]. Hemingway is an accurate chronicler, and if he has merely illustrated a change of behaviour without a simultaneous change of heart, he is illustrating the actual difference between the Paris of the 'twenties and the Spanish War of the 'thirties. The important function for a critic is to decide, not whether Hemingway has become a socialist, but whether he has given an accurate account of the changing mores of two generations. Subsequent history supports the picture Hemingway gives us. We cannot argue from Spanish examples because the Spaniard has remained clamped in a rigid situation. But the ease with which some Germans have become apparently enthusiastic communists supports Hemingway's implicit thesis, however cynical it may seem to tender susceptibilities. No one should expect a novelist to write from both the inside and the outside of his characters. If a man really believes himself to be sincere it is not part of the novelist's job to convict him from his own mouth. In other words,

[1] 'Literature and Public Events', *Penguin New Writing* No. 15.

Hemingway should not be attacked on the basis of his characters' delusions.

I am dealing with this point at some length because much criticism of Hemingway has been concentrated on it. It is a good instance of the modern habit of attacking a writer for anything but his literary skill – for his politics, his morals, his religion. I have not heard Joe Louis criticised because he did or did not attend a Peace Rally, nor has Edith Evans yet received a bad press for eating in the right or wrong restaurants. But it has become customary first of all to praise Hemingway for being an accurate reporter of an epoch and then to attack him because his reports were not always to so-and-so's liking. The trouble is (and so many people refuse to recognise this) a large proportion of the world's population has never had the barest opportunity to lead what is sometimes called 'the good life'. After the Chinese Revolution of 1911 a full democratic paraphernalia was set up – it naturally failed to work because ninety-nine per cent of the Chinese hadn't the faintest idea what it was all about. After the event wise people said it was a silly thing to do. Perhaps wise people will one day realise that unemployed men, hungry and half-clothed, cannot get excited about the great liberal aims of representative democracy and adult suffrage, secret ballot and free press (providing you have the money to institute it). The education of the *entre deux guerres* generation was badly managed. The word education has become specialised and was only applied to those who had it. The many millions who had none or were only given sufficient to fit them for work in an office or factory were not really considered. (It is like an overdressed woman going to a seaside resort where she has to fight for a deckchair and on her return saying, 'There was simply no one there, my dear, simply no one!') But there is another education, only it can be rather a sad affair, with a syllabus which has no university sanction. When war came no one asked you if you were going to participate: you were in it. These were some of the thoughts that frequently passed through Robert Jordan's mind. 'You learned the dry-mouthed, fear-purged, purging ecstasy of battle and you fought that summer and that autumn for all the things that you believed and for the new world you had been educated into.'[1] This was the situation of many men. It might be objected that Jordan was from outside, that it was no concern of his to join in this aspect of further education, and yet at the same time all the progressive voices applauded his action. Then when it is all over it is discovered that so many of his comrades, including his creator, were not genuine left-wingers, that they presumably should have kept out of a struggle for which their education had been animal and not intellectual.

Anyway, whether Hemingway was an intruder in the dust or not he is said to have raised $40,000 on personal notes to buy ambulances for Loyalist armies, and paid for them by newspaper work in Spain. I hasten to add that this has nothing to do with his literary ability. But as I am partly concerned with

[1] *For Whom the Bell Tolls.*

the personality of Hemingway as well as his skill as a writer, this fact can hardly be omitted. But on the whole I intend to concentrate personal data in a later chapter.

A much more kindly assessment of Hemingway's work in relation to political developments, particularly in Spain, was made by Arturo Barea in a review of *For Whom the Bell Tolls*. He called Hemingway 'a true man of action, yet wrestling with his very uncommunistic, honest-to-god humanist soul'.[1] This has its amusing side, for Hemingway had previously made a full-blooded attack on the humanist soul. But it says without being nasty what other writers were to say maliciously a little later – in other words, that although he could not wholeheartedly accept the communist goal or communist methods, yet he supported them temporarily because they comprised the strongest force which was fully committed to opposing something worse, Fascism. This point can be made in a number of ways. Barea does not demand that his allies should agree with him in every particular. There were others (I shall quote some presently) who condemned Hemingway for marginal differences, largely temperamental at that.

After Spain the political phase seemed to be over. Although a correspondent in the 1939 War, Hemingway often behaved more like a soldier. He thought of himself as a soldier, not really hating the enemy at all. As Robert Jordan had done in Spain, he chose his side and then did his job without the professional fierceness of a politician. The Colonel

[1] 'Not Spain But Hemingway', *Horizon*, May 1941.

in *Across the River and Into the Trees* did not in-dulge in the political self-searching of Jordan. Of course, the war was over but a large part, perhaps the greater part, of the Colonel belonged to the war. He was more concerned with strategic problems than with political morality. Like a chess player he dwelt on past campaigns, wondering where he had gone wrong, trying to assess his own actions. 'I can't hate Fascists, he thought. Nor Krauts, either, since un-fortunately I am a soldier.' Perhaps he had never hated Fascists. But we must not fall into the trap of watching Jake Barnes become Robert Jordan be-come the Colonel. It is sometimes a useful hypothesis but it must not be treated as infallible. When the night porter at the hotel says to the Colonel, 'I have so little political development that I believe all honourable men are honourable', he may be voicing his creator's opinion. It rather sounds like it. The Colonel replies with a cynical joke that suggests he no longer takes any serious interest in politics, but knows that he must accept its experience. However much you may proclaim that there are good men on all sides and it is better for all the good men to agree than to fight each other, the parties will still continue to exist and new ones to be formed and the good men to divide themselves among them.

In Spain Robert Jordan had seen how crooked even the best politics are. Thinking about the times he had been to Gaylord's in Madrid he realised that his education had taken another step forward there. 'Sure, Gaylord's was the place you needed to com-plete your education. It was there you learned how it was all really done instead of how it was supposed to be done. He had only started his education, he thought.'[1] The sensible attitude to adopt was to regard politics, with its manœuvring and juggling, as a necessity in the world as it was. There had to be organisation, organisation had to be controlled by men, and there weren't enough saints to go round. Once you recognised this you didn't feel uncomfortable when you discovered corruption and dishonesty on your side; you knew it was inevitable and through this knowledge you yourself actually became more reliable because, unlike the innocent idealist, you didn't retire in disgust before your job was finished. But when it was you were at perfect liberty to step aside and let them carry on without you. That seemed to be the lesson of Gaylord's.

But despite this knowledge and resignation it was impossible to resist twinges of bitterness. Even if you recognised that human beings were so foolish they were condemned to be ruled by the worst, knowing it did not make the fact pleasant. When Renata asked her Colonel why he wasn't President of the United States she was probably surprised by the outburst the question elicited:

> Me President? I served in the Montana National Guard when I was sixteen. But I never wore a bow tie in my life and I am not, nor ever have been, an unsuccessful haberdasher. I have none of the qualifications for the Presidency. I couldn't even head the opposition even though I don't have to sit on telephone books to have my picture taken. Nor am

[1] *For Whom the Bell Tolls.*

I a no-fight general. Hell, I never even was at SHAEF I couldn't even be an elder statesman. I'm not old enough. Now we are governed in some way, by the dregs. We are governed by what you find in the bottom of dead beer glasses that whores have dunked their cigarettes in. The place has not even been swept out yet and they have an amateur pianist beating on the box.[1]

But if this is an American Colonel on the fifty mark, Hemingway himself has also gone on record. Interviewed by Harvey Breit of the *New York Times* he is alleged to have said:

> 'All the contact I have had with it [politics] has left me feeling as though I had been drinking out of spittoons. The self-confessed patriot, the traitor and the regulator of other people's lives, beliefs, etc., and the Regimentator all run in a photo-finish. The Senate may develop the picture if they can find a photographer who can photograph a photo-finish.'[2]

This is probably final. Animal back to animal, some would say, but it is a more complicated development than that. Circumstances caused the man who had written of a generation devoted to sensation to enter the political arena and to take his characters with him. What they saw they did not like and when the opportune moment arrived they resigned membership. But they could not return to where they had come from. The Lost Generation was now Dead. The Lost Generation had not even considered political solutions — in fact, they did not look for solutions at all. Now, considerably older, they have

[1] *Across the River.*   [2] *The New York Times*, 17 Sept. 1950.

experienced and rejected a large sector of human activity and behaviour. There is left love and duck-shooting and the other preoccupations of Jake Barnes, but they are the residue not of indifference but of experience. Edwin Muir might say I told you so but he could not say they had been wrong.

Hemingway's war experience and, by implication, the Colonel's of *Across the River* were not simply products of lust, aggressiveness and animal instinct. They were the fruit of cool and deliberate thinking. Neither were adventurers like Frederick Henry merely wanting to taste adventure and see death close up. They made definite, unqualified Yes-No decisions, and then did what was expected of them, modified by temperament. As we have seen, even Robert Jordan was at this stage and there was no retreat from it. So were the partisans he worked with. Killing was not a pleasure or a mechanical response to stimuli, but a duty. The only people who retained the old joy in killing were the gypsies. Anselmo made this clear in a conversation with Jordan:

'The gypsies have many laws they do not admit to having. In the war many gypsies have become bad again as they were in the olden times.'
'They do not understand why the war is made. They do not know for what we fight.'
'No,' Anselmo said. 'They only know now there is a war and people may kill again as in the olden times without a surety of punishment.'[1]

There is an enormous difference between the

[1] *For Whom the Bell Tolls.*

sobriety of Robert Jordan, the partisans and the Colonel and the messianic quality of the old revolutionaries who believed that a little shooting would bring the New World. The Italian socialists were gay and confident in their innocence. It was not till a war of revolutionary significance should be fought that they would discover that revolution was neither joyful nor certain. Mr. Frazer, lying in his wheeled chair, had seen a long time ago in a moment of vision what the idea of revolution conveyed to simple people. 'Revolution, Mr. Frazer thought, is no opium. Revolution is a catharsis; an ecstasy which can only be prolonged by tyranny.'[1] But when you fought in your own right, when the tyranny had been temporarily removed and replaced by one of your own, the ecstasy died.

Because Hemingway could not give full intellectual allegiance to the Republicans in Spain he was attacked by those who did not share his doubts. By the familiar process of hundredpercentism (i.e., if you are not X you must be Y) it was decided that in fact *For Whom the Bell Tolls* was sympathetic to Fascism. An example of this is to be found in a book by Berry Burgum, who reached a 'surprisingly definite conclusion'. A sensitive reader 'would have perceived that it accomplishes precisely the opposite from what it intended, that it is derogatory to the cause of Spanish democracy, and therefore, by implication, sympathetic to Spanish fascism.'[2] Because

[1] 'Gambler, Nun and Radio', from *Winner Take Nothing*.
[2] *The Novel and the World's Dilemma*.

Robert Jordan decided that, as an officer, he must obey his orders irrespective of his personal qualms, Burgum declares that 'the psychology of Robert Jordan is, I should say, strangely enough that typical of the authoritarianism of fascism'. There is a case for giving the soldier in a 'free army' more scope for personal initiative, but as armies, revolutionary and fascist and democratic, are at present constituted it would be risking court martial and possible sentence of death to indulge such individual thinking. I don't know why Burgum expects others to take such risks. Surely that is a matter for one's own conscience only. The fault lies not with the individual soldier, who is rarely a fanatic[1], however sincere he may be, but with the hierarchy that imposes a set of regulations on him.

In 1935, twelve years before this attack, a Russian critic had berated Hemingway for his 'bourgeois individualism'. While the former aesthetes had become radicals, visited the mining districts of Kentucky and joined writers' committees, ending up as 'proletarians of art', devoting their energies to the prosecution of the class struggle, Hemingway had degenerated from being the pet of American youth, then spokesman of the Lost Generation, to being a maniac and eventually coming to rest as a degenerate.[2] These terms are typical of 'marxist' criticism

[1] 'Fanatics do not make good friends for a cause.' Ernest Hemingway, Preface to The Fifth Column.
[2] J. Kashkeen, 'Ernest Hemingway: A Tragedy of Craftsmanship', from Ernest Hemingway: The Man and His Work, ed. McCaffery.

and need not be taken too seriously. But in their milder way Western critics also trounced Hemingway in print for not being copies of themselves.

Reading some of these attacks one might get the impression that Hemingway is a fearsome barbarian who first tried to debauch American youth and then became a fifth column ally of Fascism because he did not dare to admit his contempt for the proletariat. It is very easy to pass from good sense to sheer fantasy by easy stages without noticing the change. There are few rules to criticism but surely one is that a man must be judged by his work. You must believe what a man writes unless there is a clear and positive reason for disbelief. There are many writers who have dared to state publicly that they prefer Fascism to Socialism, among them de Montherlant and Wyndham Lewis. There is no suggestion in either his life or work that Hemingway had not the courage to say this also if he was of the same opinion. The truth is surely that he has never been an advocate of Fascism (even if most of his beloved bullfighters did join the Fascists when the fighting started and even if he had more in common with Marinetti than with Sydney Webb), nor has he attacked the ideals of Socialism. He has attacked the methods, as even the most loyal socialist must. It is not good criticism to judge a man by what he doesn't write, according to nuances which often only exist in the mind of the critic. The regulated life of socialism will be harder for some to accept than for others. So is marriage. But in neither case does difficulty of adjustment imply opposition.

I once wrote a letter to Hemingway asking him to answer some rather stupid questions. All blanket questions to writers are stupid but the alternative is to ask none at all. If the questions are stupid it does not mean that the answers will be, especially when they don't answer the question put. When I asked Hemingway something about the future of sensibility he replied that there is a future for little else 'except the fundamental conception of individual freedom and liberty and the universal brotherhood of man'. I don't know whether he has ever expressed himself in such generalities before. Anyway, that's what he says and no examination of his text, however close, will wipe it out.

N.B. I don't know whether this story has any relevance. I think it may. A friend once remarked to Koussevitzky when he was rehearsing the Fantastic Symphony that there was a great deal of bombast in Berlioz's score. Koussevitzky looked pained and said, 'Even if it is so, I don't want to discuss it. I must not think of defects when I play the music.' Criticism has become a *searching* for defects: they should only be noticed when they are obtrusive. Then the work should be rejected. It is the good we're looking for.

CHAPTER III

MIRROR OF SOCIETY

FIRST of all, despite the Lost Generation and the killers and the dubious revolutionaries and the inarticulate human beings, let us regard Hemingway as a recording instrument. He put down what he saw, just as Conrad did, and also what he heard. His subject was society, and although he influenced society or a section of it this was a by-product, for his intention had been artistic not moralistic. If Hemingway had not been such a powerful writer, gathering disciples he never knew as he progressed, no one would have troubled to have scrutinised the opinions of his characters so closely. Henry Seidel Canby, introducing the Modern Library edition of *The Sun Also Rises*[1], said the novel, 'among other things, is an example of first-rate reporting'. This is not the whole story but the rest is feeling and understanding, not didacticism. The reading public turned *For Whom the Bell Tolls* into a partly didactic novel. In the intellectual climate of that time a first-rate writer hardly dared to stand aside. Stephen Spender had the right idea when he wrote that Hemingway is 'corrupt in his values to the extent that his age is corrupt'.[2] Even so, this can still be only a half-truth. Because Hemingway did not write

[1] *Fiesta* in England.
[2] 'Literature and Public Events', *Penguin New Writing*, No. 15.

of the Lost Generation in terms of horror (which would quickly become boring) it is wrong to assume that he accepted their values or lack of values.

I can best illustrate the point of this short happy chapter by reference to the short happy life of Francis Macomber. The dominant figure is neither Macomber nor his wife, but Wilson, the white hunter, who, like a bullfighter, knew his job and only sought excellence in it. But it was an unusual kind of job, taking rich people into bush or savannah and helping them to shoot big game and, above all, persuading them they did it well, perhaps better than anyone else. Besides technical skill it required tact. His clientele was an odd minority of the human race, the very rich and usually dissatisfied. He had to be prepared for anything that might happen – cowardice, for instance, or, in his own phrase, a windfall. Mrs. Macomber, ashamed of her husband, was a windfall and made it clear that she wished to fall into Wilson's doublesize cot. Wilson might have refused. He might have said: This is not part of my contract, or I disapprove of promiscuity, but in fact he accepted. 'Their standards were his standards as long as they were hiring him.'[1]

Wilson adapted himself to the tiny society he moved in. He had to make a living and he could not afford to antagonise his clients. A creative writer must make a similar accommodation with his material, not necessarily in his life (though if the divorce is too great there will be no material to work upon, except by reflection) but certainly in the commodities

[1] 'The Short Happy Life of Francis Macomber'.

of his artistic experience. He must accept to a very large extent. I doubt if any good novel has come out of rejection pure and simple. *Darkness at Noon* comes out of rejection, but the rejection came out of a fierce acceptance. We must always come back to this truth, that a creative writer must participate in the events of life as a merchant does in the sale of commodities and not as a priest does in the conflict of values. It is not his job to cure like the doctor but it must not be too easily assumed that if the writer shows no apparent concern with salvation he is therefore seeking destruction. The most disgusting picture of society that Hemingway has given us is to be found in *To Have and Have Not*, but we should not hastily conclude that Hemingway enjoyed the spectacle. In fact it is obvious that he found it nauseating in general, though he may have felt a strong regard for some of its aspects, particularly those where weak men fought courageously against great odds. Introducing a book of essays on Hemingway, McCaffery wrote that this novel 'is an extraordinary recreation of the chaos, brutality and fear of a society on the edge of an abyss'[1]. He quotes Aquinas on art: 'the right disposition toward a true end', and asks what other disposition or form suited 1932 but formlessness.

Looking into this novel, which the critics found more distasteful than anything else Hemingway had written, we find ourselves presented with two nations. First we meet the poor, many of them vici-

[1] *Ernest Hemingway: The Man and His Work*, ed. McCaffery.

ous, but presumably vicious because they are poor. Then, with a sudden switch for which we are not prepared, the rich – most of them vicious because they are rich. From this point the two are contrasted, and the sordidness of the poor is a constant background to the rottenness of the rich. This is a new vision for Hemingway. We did not get it at all in the first two novels. It is not a good novel for several reasons, but one of them is that the author's anger boils over and he starts throwing insults around. He does not do it by sociological essay in the manner of Dos Passos or Steinbeck, but his selection is so partial the effect is similar. In this novel he tells us more directly than in any other how rotten society is. The expatriates had been responsible to no one but themselves and it was their own affair how they went to hell, but now he is writing of people who cause suffering and misery to other people through the machinery of their dubious pleasure-seeking. The social message is loud but the organism is weak. The connecting links between the two groups are shown only on the physical (or more truly, nocturnal) plane. But that need not concern us. All I wish to state now is that Hemingway presents us with a situation and his literary devices grow out of the situation. Anger echoes anger; chaos, chaos.

But there is a passage where the biological closeness between the two groups is unexpectedly revealed. The novelist Richard Gordon and his wife, junior members of the privileged class, are having a sex quarrel. She accuses him of 'changing your politics to suit the fashion, sucking up to people's faces and talking about them behind their backs'. He's a nasty little sycophant and she's sick of him. Attacking his pretensions, she forgets hers and suddenly lays bare her social background. 'My father wore wool socks and put his feet in them upon a chair and read the paper in the evening. And when we had croup he took care of us. He was a boiler maker and his hands were all broken and he liked to fight when he drank and he could fight when he was sober.'[1]

Here and in other places what Hemingway is hinting at is that the truly horrible, anti-human fault in society is not its division into rich and poor, strong and weak, honest and dishonest, but into pretentious and unpretentious.[2] As one by one of the wealthy characters, the heiresses and company promoters and film actresses, are stripped bare we see what messy and unattractive creatures they are. They have nothing to be proud of. The public sees their masks and shams and inventions but underneath are things which have to be hidden – drugs, masturbation, homosexuality. Harry Morgan, on the other side of the fence, has little but what he has is good. This great gulf opens up and it is described so brutally we can be forgiven for believing that Hemingway has just seen it for the first time. But if he becomes a moralist in this novel and chooses the

[1] *To Have and Have Not.*
[2] Affectation usually forms part of pretentiousness. Part I of *The Torrents of Spring* is prefaced by this quotation from Fielding. 'The only source of the true Ridiculous (as it appears to me) is affectation.'

healthy animal becoming vaguely political, he presents an even more horrible alternative. He reflects a society torn down the middle, suggests a preference – and stops. He catalogues the victims of financial speculation and the various interesting ways in which they can die.

> Some made the long drop from the apartment or the office window; some took it quietly in two-car garages with the motor running; some used the native tradition of the Colt or Smith and Wesson; those well constructed implements that end insomnia, terminate remorse, cure cancer, avoid bankruptcy, and blast an exit from intolerable positions by the pressure of a finger; those admirable American instruments so easily carried, so sure of effect, so well designed to end the American dream when it becomes a nightmare, their only drawback the mess they leave for relatives to clear up.

Such a society is utterly merciless and, in accordance with it, so is Hemingway's treatment. Yet at the same time he avoids the sentimentality of the tough writer (for instance, Hodding Carter) who wallows in the very thing he believes he is avoiding.[1]

I have stated that this consciousness of background is not present in the two earlier novels. They are minor actions, taking place in isolation, whereas *To Have and Have Not* attempts to relate the specific time and place to the world at large. Yet it was not Hemingway's first effort to supply a background

[1] Muir's charge of sentimentality is not the same. I am referring to the deliberate bottling up of felt emotion, so that it comes out in disguise. Hemingway manages to numb his emotions to that they are not involved.

to his action. In his first book of stories *In Our Time*, each story was prefaced by an epigraph, ostensibly unrelated to the rest of the book or each other, yet providing snapshots of the world behind. The difference between these and the background of *To Have and Have Not* is that they showed no social concern. Without exception they were vignettes of war and violence, brutality and bullring. But the urge to make the work in hand an integral part of the whole was apparent. As a device it was nearly new. The only earlier example I can think of is Hardy's *The Dynasts* where worldwide events are played as in a theatre to an audience of critical spirits. Hemingway leaves criticism to the reader.

Now we come to the Humanist (whom Hemingway calls an 'extinct phenomenon', but his extinction is recent and possibly hastened by Hemingway himself). According to Hemingway it was the Humanist who objected to his close study of men and women. The Humanist believed in the more kindly virtues and then proceeded to turn away from the baser qualities. If you see brutality, insincerity or selfishness in the world, they seemed to say, it is best to ignore them. If you don't you will be tainted. Also if you don't you will probably be suspected of admiring them, observing them for their own sake. The basis of Humanism may be Hedonism, which in my view is a perfectly respectable attitude to life. But it is not an artist's attitude, though an artist may indulge in it when he is not thinking of his art. Hemingway gets great fun out of the Humanist's predicament.

In my musings as a naturalist it has occurred to me
that while decorum is an excellent thing some must be
indecorous if the race is to be carried on since the
position prescribed for procreation is indecorous,
highly indecorous, and it occurred to me that perhaps
that is what these people are, or were: the children
of decorous cohabitation.[1]

This is a nice parallel: we must be indecorous to
prolong life and Hemingway will be indecorous to
prolong literature. After all, there are already enough
people writing essays on the End of the Novel.

Edmund Wilson has called Hemingway a Gauge
of Morale. 'His whole work is a criticism of society:
he has responded to every pressure of the moral atmosphere of the time, as it is felt at the roots of human
relations, with a sensitivity almost unrivalled. Even
his preoccupation with licking the gang in the next
block and being known as the best basketball player
in high school has its meaning in the present epoch.'[2]
The moral atmosphere is what Bernard Shaw called
Anarchism. It is plugged like a dance tune but insid-
iously and it creeps into every crevice like a vapour.
'The doctrine with which Hollywood is corrupting
the world,' Shaw wrote, 'is the doctrine of Anarchism.
Hollywood keeps before its child audiences a string
of glorified young heroes, every one of whom is an un-
hesitating and violent young Anarchist. His one
answer to everything that annoys him or disparages
his country or his parents or his young lady or his
personal code of manly conduct, is to give the offender

[1] *Death in the Afternoon.*
[3] *The Wound and the Bow.*

a sock in the jaw.'[1] Hollywood 'glorifies' the doctrine. (It is not actually the doctrine of Anarchism, which has been elaborated and institutionalised, but a kind of anarchistic emanation.) Hemingway doesn't glorify, although he comes near to it in the case of Harry Morgan, but in this case he has the excuse of reaction from a worse alternative. He gets inside the moral atmosphere of his time in order to give us its full flavour. He has done what Fielding did in the eighteenth century but with the greater freedom of the twentieth century, he has not felt it necessary to stop periodically and exclaim how shocking, disgusting, wicked, immoral and shameless are certain characters and certain actions.

One of the characteristics of our civilisation is the way barbarism is overpowering it from within. The last comparable victory of barbarism, which took place during the later stages of the Roman Empire, was a victory of external forces. Culture was not changed or diluted but swamped. It is impossible to say today who are the cultured classes. It is more likely that no such classes exist, or if they do that they are weakened and impoverished and are being remorselessly ground out of existence. Only solitary individuals remain. Even before the war it was possible to find places in London where civilised people congregated during their leisure hours. Now these groups have been fragmented and communication has practically broken down. The yellow press and strip cartoons are read as avidly by so-called educated people as by the mass. The percentage of trash put

[1] *The Political Madhouse in America and Nearer Home.*

out by publishing houses is greater than at any previous time I have evidence of. It is becoming more and more difficult to make a film in which any appeal other than box-office is made. Books are bought by libraries, not by individuals – and in a society based on the publication of the printed word it is the possession of books that creates a cultured climate, not the memory of them. When the present revolution is complete and the only remaining books will be textbooks on microfilm, the new form of communication on which the next phase will be based, television, will be firmly in the hands of the barbarians. It is useless for us to compare the early printers and booksellers with the modern television sponsor.

This degeneration is a pretty accurate reflection of the social scene in general – and the literary world has not always reflected society faithfully. Having ridiculed the Victorians and punctured the Great Literary Idols we are beginning to see that the wall they erected had its uses. The Victorians were always frightened by the possible eruption of the submerged tenth. We are witnessing it today. Instead of raising his hands in horror Hemingway soberly wrote it down. I said before that he could, in certain moods, have gone for a walk with Wordsworth. He could have taken another one with Mayhew. There is one little incident in Hemingway's life, entirely unimportant in itself, which caught my imagination like a sunset. It comes from the *New Yorker* profile by Lillian Ross and before I quote it I had better say that if an Oscar were ever awarded for unashamed prejudice and even malice Lillian Ross would run

Ehrenburg close. Perhaps some people reinforce their egos by finding faults in the acknowledged great (the comforting doctrine that we are all very much alike really). Only a few years ago some reviewers were made immensely happy by the discovery that Ruskin behaved badly to his wife. We learn from Miss Ross that Hemingway is really just a retarded adolescent. Therefore we must treat this little incident with caution. It may be Miss Ross's fun.

Hemingway called on his publisher, Charles Scribner. There followed the following conversation.

'We've been looking at pictures, Charlie,' Hemingway said as he went up the elevator. 'They have some pretty good pictures now, Charlie.'

Scribner nodded and said. 'Yuh, yuh.'

'Was fun for country boy like me,' Hemingway said.

'Yuh, yuh,' said Scribner.[1]

I'd much prefer it on better authority, but this snatch of conversation between a great novelist and a great publisher has a genuine twentieth-century ring. I could imagine that Hemingway's country-boy remark was a little joke. I made a similar one once to a Cabinet Minister's wife and she laughed, so it couldn't be that bad. But what would Byron's Murray have made of those 'Yuh, yuhs'?

It is generally agreed that our society is one of the most materialist in history. There are good *a priori* grounds for believing this likely. It is only in recent times that mass production and high pressure advertising have made abundant goods available

[1] *The New Yorker*, 13 May 1950.

and, more important, told everyone that they ought to possess them. There was little money in circulation during the Middle Ages because there was nothing much to buy with it (you can only eat a limited amount of food and sit in one chair at a time). When trade and industry developed, money followed. Today there is a furious compulsion to acquire money, not yet restrained in America and growing enormously in Asia, so that everyone can have his own car and television set and refrigerator and, shortly, helicopter. Sociologists constantly remark on this trend in sober, documented studies. Hemingway gives the raw material – and the astonishing thing is that the very people who generalise and rationalise the process object strongly to direct presentation. It is felt that to describe a thing indirectly is socially safe. Tell people that sin is unpleasant and they will believe you. Make the sin actually appear unpleasant and they will surrender to its charms. This is the paradox of the opposition to Hemingway.

In 'A Clean, Well-Lighted Place' he reports two waiters discussing one of their regular customers.

> 'Last week he tried to commit suicide', one waiter said.
> 'Why?'
> 'He was in despair'.
> 'What about?'
> 'Nothing'.
> 'How do you know it was nothing?'
> 'He has plenty of money'.[1]

Now I can imagine no one objecting to this in

[1] From *Winner Take Nothing*.

itself, though many would deplore the implied philosophy. Yet in the whole of his treatment of modern society Hemingway does no more than this. He does not tell us that some people believe that it is impossible for a rich man to be unhappy; he shows the belief in action. And it is very significant that one of the first lessons our moralising parents and tutors teach us in our good Christian homes is that money is not of first importance. It comes after honesty, truthfulness, generosity and many other virtues. Although the tone of our society is naked and unashamed it is immoral to look at it. It is the Humanist again, turning away from the sores in the hope that they will heal by themselves. And if we look at something that is as large as the landscape itself we are labelled *voyeurs* and Peeping Toms.

Once these ideas get a foothold in the mind it seems almost impossible to drive them out. Most people are mentally lazy and this is equally true of sociologists and literary critics. They expend their energy during youth and live the rest of their lives on the capital of one idea, or two if they're very clever. Just as there is a communal *idée fixe* about the effect of realism and naturalism on the reader (particularly those who don't read books anyway) so there is an undying picture of the Lost Generation which still crops up in studies of the period. Bill Gorton himself could have written a book about his own alleged decadence. 'You're an expatriate. You've lost touch with the soil. You get precious. Fake European standards have ruined you. You drink yourself to death. You become obsessed by sex. You spend all your time talking, not working. You are an expatriate, see? You hang around cafés.'[1] And people still sum them up in this way, forgetting that among them were Hemingway and FitzGerald and Pound and Joyce and Ford and Dos Passos and Cummings, to name the writers only. The people in *Fiesta* are among the most attractive in modern fiction, along with George Sherston. But there are still people who believe that Kaiser Wilhelm was solely responsible for World War I; that all Jews have hooked noses; that black men have thicker skulls than white men, who need topees; that pregnant women cause meat to go bad, which may be true; and the other day a lady told me it is useless giving baths to the poor as they will keep their coal in them.

We now recognise in Hemingway a chronicler of the period. I hope it is not straining a parallel too much to call him a Froissart. Despite the gap of centuries, there is some wonderfully fresh and exact description in the mediaeval writer which seems to anticipate Hemingway. But having thrown the image at the public, Hemingway must have been surprised to find it being transformed into an idol. Literature is never exact reflection, of course. It is the author's selection that forms the art. But in this case there was a secondary selection, made by the younger generation looking for a model. 'Hemingway, as Lord Byron had done a century before, gave the young people attitudes to strike and patterns of conduct to follow. They not only wrote like him, if they wrote, and walked with his rolling slouch if they had seen

[1] *Fiesta.*

him, but also drank like his heroes and heroines, culti-
vated a hard-boiled melancholy and talked in page
after page of Hemingway dialogue.'[1] Hemingway had
chosen the significant elements of the society he lived
in, and those young people of Europe and America
who read books chose the elements that appealed to
them for their own use. But more than the life portrayed, although that was exciting and valid for them,
it was the style that took their fancy. It was because
he had a style to offer (and a manageable one, unlike
Joyce's) that Hemingway became the most influential
man of his time, outstripping T. E. Lawrence who
demanded too much and W. H. Auden, whose appeal
was too limited.

[1] 'A Portrait of Mr. Papa', by Malcolm Cowley, from
Ernest Hemingway: the Man and his Work, ed. McCaffery.

CHAPTER IV

THAT FAMOUS STYLE

THERE was once a man who decided to become the world's greatest critic. The first mistake he made was to read all the great books while he was too young. Realising that he would never have time to read them again, and beginning to suffer from indigestion anyway, he marked certain passages and jotted clever remarks at the end. Whenever he needed to refer to a particular work it was easy to find his way about – but the way was frozen and the traveller was of necessity permanently immature. But new books kept appearing and it was necessary to read them all because everyone cried for his opinion. In the end he found it agony to read but he was too set to change his habits. This was the dilemma of the World's Greatest Critic. He became self-conscious and professionalised and he would have been happier as an engineer. Moral: always work out of love or, if you find my terms embarrassing, out of sympathy. Modern criticism is usually written out of hate, smeared with a pretence of affection, particularly when the critic is compelled by financial reasons to say how wonderful a book is.

* * * * *

Hemingway's fame was won largely by the simplicity of his style, which some call deceptive, meaning the ease is in the reading not in the writing.

Simple writing is the hard way, leaving the author naked.

> If a man writes clearly enough anyone can see if he fakes. If he mystifies to avoid a straight statement, which is very different from breaking so-called rules of syntax or grammar to make an effect which can be obtained in no other way, the writer takes a longer time to be known as a fake and other writers who are afflicted by the same necessity will praise him in their own defence[1].

He concludes: 'all bad writers are in love with the epic'.

It is the absorption in things in themselves (which I illustrated in the first chapter) that marked Hemingway off from his predecessors and most of his contemporaries. There is never any feeling of strain, any suspicion that a description is a nicely planned piece of symbolism. Often, of course, it is symbolic – but always out of its own trueness. It is symbolic in the way that life itself can suddenly become symbolic, leading to a belief in omens and a directing power who warns those who have the wit to understand. But classical symbolism, which persisted till a very late day even among the best novelists and is still part of the stock-in-trade of the others, is rarely to be found in Hemingway's work. There is a surprising example in 'The Snows of Kilimanjaro', where a man is dying and 'death had come and rested its head on the foot of the cot and he could smell its breath'. This is so unusual in Hemingway the reader cannot dispel the

---

[1] *Death in the Afternoon.*

suspicion that after all there must have been something real that really smelt. Even Hemingway must
have been amazed by this intrusion of an alien sentiment for he hastily adds (in the dying man's words)
that death needn't be a skeleton with a scythe but
might just as easily be two bicycle policemen or a bird.

Reviewing *The Sun Also Rises* on its first publication the *Nation* wrote: 'his perception of the
physical object is direct and accurate; his vision of
character singularly oblique'. This dualism is most
marked in all the early work, up to and including
To Have and Have Not, though in this novel a dilu-
tion has already begun. Hemingway keeps both eyes
on the object and half an eye on the man: but his
ears are wide open. The Russian critic J. Kashkeen
refers to a theory of 'expressive suggestion'.[1] The
suggestion is twofold, and its action corresponds to
the difference in material, human and non-human.
As is well known, the accumulation of external details conveys a mood, a mood which the sensibility
of the reader picks up like a radio receiver. He gets
no direct assistance from the author. But the reality
of the characters is conveyed by a directly opposite
method. They are never described in the same de-
tailed way. It is impossible to think of a Hemingway
character and describe his appearance with any certainty. We are given his mannerisms of gesture,
perhaps, but more usually of speech. There is no
struggle with the author as happens so often when
reading novelists of the past, where a personal image

[1] 'A Tragedy of Craftsmanship', *Ernest Hemingway: the
Man and his Work*, ed. McCaffery.

conflicts with the carefully delineated image presented by his creator. Hemingway allows us to share in creation, we finish out of our own experience the sketch he has begun.

So many of the details appear to be unnecessary. It is a sudden word or phrase that suddenly blends them into a comprehensible whole. The reader must have the sensibility or, in some cases, the experience to grasp the key. It is not always accessible. It is very much an esoteric literature in this sense. Also it is no adverse criticism of a reader if he does not grasp the key – it may belong to a sphere of living in which he has never participated. For this reason a reader may be justified in claiming that Hemingway is deliberately obscure. I know for myself that stories which were once incomprehensible to me have after some years become little masterpieces because in the meantime I have broadened my experience and been able to connect the fragments in a meaningful way. 'Hills Like White Elephants'[1] comes beautifully to life when one unspoken word is excavated from the raw material. The girl's irritability is contrasted with the man's pathetic anxiety to please, and there is no resolution. There is to be an operation. The story ends with the girl saying she feels fine and our knowing that the squabble will break out again in a very short time. Also that the girl is right when she says the operation will change nothing. But it is not a trivial difference of opinion that lies between them. The unnamed operation is abortion and the immense pathos of this story comes from our knowledge that

[1] From *Men Without Women*.

the man's optimism is blind and even cheerless and that the girl is being persuaded to deny herself the one experience that might save her.

There are always readers who will ask: Is the obscurity justified by the effect? They are usually people who find satisfaction in the patterned stories of O. Henry and de Maupassant. Hemingway's defence could be that as he deliberately sets out to give as close a rendering of life through the medium of words as is possible, he could not honestly write in any other way. People very often do not name the most important things in their lives, though they may refer to them continually. Life is not arranged in self-contained episodes and even when old people profess to see a plan which contains the whole of their past experience and is being brought to its completion, it is fairly certain that such a plan is a psychological construct which ignores, thanks to a convenient memory, all unassimilable data. Hemingway's stories do not please the architects among us. Instead they give a sense of life as chaotic as experience itself. We should always be on the lookout for literary rationalisation, too. The desire for innovation usually arises out of intense boredom. Hemingway started writing his stories at a time when the old plot genre had become so widespread and familiar that everyone who used a pen could put a competent story together with considerable technical skill (according to the standards of the day) and a complete absence of poetic thrill. Boredom and a cracking culture are a powerful combination.

Seeing and Hearing

It is impossible to discuss Hemingway's style without considering the verbal-emotional discipline which is its central feature. This style appears so casual, so careless. Yet it has enormous personality. Now this personality is not the careful creation of a Flaubert, for although Hemingway works hard on his scripts it is impossible to simulate carelessness and indifference. They are self-existing qualities, part of life and essential to poetry. It is less his art than his poetry that distinguishes Hemingway. It is by training his poetic instinct to one end alone that he enables it to produce its full effect. This aim lies in the reproduction only of what he sees and hears. He followed Conrad who insisted on putting down what he saw and never what his intellect inferred. (For instance, looking over the side of his ship he saw a headless body because the head was out of sight.) Hemingway is at the other extreme from Scott who described landscapes on a level of unchanging monotony. He always wrote down what he knew to be there, never simply what he saw. When he is not interested in a scene Hemingway dismisses it with a few words, giving a generalised impression – anonymous people in an anonymous street, undifferentiated masses of green on a brown hillside. But as soon as his interest becomes engaged his senses become alert and we are presented with the details in all their sharp actuality. On a journey men miss many things but on arrival their apprehension is specific and total.

As John Lehmann once wrote, you do not need

a university education to get the full flavour from Hemingway.[1] He has retained the ordinary man's way of looking at things which is rare in a writer. Neither education nor professional pride have persuaded him to wallow in the inessential, one of the major faults of our literature. Yet the charge against him has been that he cannot distinguish between the relevant and the irrelevant. The truth is that what is irrelevant to the academically-trained mind is not the same as that seen by the untrained mind. Writing of the latter he adopts its methods and viewpoints.

Many people who insist that he cannot write (omitting to add 'like Forster or Henry James' which is what they really mean) still admit that he is a master of dialogue. 'But, you say, there is very little dialogue in this book. Why isn't there more dialogue? What we want in a book by this citizen is people talking; that is all he knows how to do and now he doesn't do it.'[2] Hemingway takes immense trouble with his dialogue. It's got to sound right – which isn't the same as saying it must be an exact transcription. Sam Boal describes how, when he has finished his day's work, Hemingway insists on reading it over to anyone who can be pressed into service – usually his wife, but it may be an utterly unliterary guest (better for Hemingway's purposes, anyway). The reading is punctuated by questions: 'That sound right? Hit your ears right? People talk that way?'[3] This is the technical illustration of the intellectual criticism that

[1] *New Writing in Europe.*
[3] *Death in the Afternoon.*
[2] 'I Tell You True', *Park East*, December 1950.

Hemingway's appeal is solely to the senses. He writes from the senses and is biology talking.

Yet his dialogue is not as naturalistic as some critics would have us believe. One of the greatest dangers of all assessment of imponderables is the attraction of extreme attitudes. We have seen that, for not being wholeheartedly communist, Hemingway has been dismissed as a fascist. For concentrating on sensation he has been damned as incapable of thought. And now, in the case of his dialogue, because he writes by ear he is accused of a naturalism that never was and never could be. Not even Dorothy Richardson could have put down everything that Hemingway was supposed to have recorded in his infatuation for exact reporting. Take any novel, particularly one of the early ones of which the charge was made, and test the dialogue. There is more missing than is present. One thing any novelist must learn to control is a sense of time – the specious time of the novel must have an emotional equivalent to the actual time of the clock. A good working test of a novelist's ability is contained in this rule. If after two pages the author announces that an hour has passed and you are held up by a sense of unreality, the author has failed. When you do not question the hour but accept it immediately, he has succeeded. Hemingway nearly always passes this test. Success is controlled by selection, by repetition and colloquial rhythm. It is this rhythm that Hemingway captures in the case of Jake Barnes and Lieutenant Henry and their associates, the individual flavour of their speech, and their methods of expression. But when he has made the selection which presents in a living way the essential core of speech, it has to be right, truly heard and accurately ordered. The pattern is never imposed from outside. There is none of the proletarian novelist's trick of making characters speak as they ought to speak. His dialogues give an 'impression of freshness, even in monotony'.[1]

As he developed, sometimes appearing to go backward as he tried to go forward, the early nature of this dialogue changed, though subtly. In the following passage from *To Have and Have Not* we get the short crisp statement and mechanical repartee that Jake Barnes and Bill Gorton made famous but it has an additional brusqueness and crudity.

> As they came out Albert came up to the place and went up to Harry.
>
> 'I'm sorry, Albert, I can't use you', Harry said. He had thought it out that far already.
>
> 'I'd go cheap', Albert said.
>
> 'I'm sorry', Harry said. 'I got no need for you now'.
>
> 'You won't get a good man for what I'd go for', Albert said.
>
> 'I'm going by myself'.
>
> 'You don't want to make a trip like that alone', Albert said.
>
> 'Shut up', said Harry. 'What do you know about it? Do they teach you my business on the relief?'
>
> 'Go to hell', said Albert.
>
> 'Maybe I will', said Harry. Anyone looking at him could tell he was thinking plenty fast and he did not want to be bothered.
>
> 'I'd like to go', Albert said.

[1] Mario Praz, 'Hemingway in Italy', *Partisan Review*, Oct. 1948.

'I can't use you', Harry said. 'Let me alone, will you?'

The difference between the tone of this and of the dialogue in the earlier novels is due more to a change of scene than a change in the author. Although Albert and Harry are technically friends there is no love between them. There was real love between Jake Barnes and Bill Gorton. The surprising thing about *Fiesta*, considering its reputation as a novel portraying the failure of love to realise itself, is the amount of love that does in fact exist between Jake and Brett and Bill and Mike. But owing to the change in the social climate which we have already examined and Hemingway's realisation that, to keep pace with the world and even the characters he had created he must adjust himself to that climate, we get the new tone of *To Have and Have Not* with its hardness and asperity. One great difference is that the new characters are too tense to make fun of each other. In *Fiesta* they found it difficult not to.

Nick, Jake, Brett et Alia

Very few novelists have been really successful in creating a complete character who develops a life of his own so that he exists outside the book like an absent acquaintance. Characterisation has never been Hemingway's strongest point. If we can actually hear his people speak we cannot always see them act – certainly not as vividly as we see the battlefield after the battle or the preparations for a meal by the river. His earliest attempts were not at all successful. Nick

Adams and his friend Bill are so much alike, sharing thoughts, books and actions to such a degree they have no individuality. There is an advance in *Fiesta* and *Farewell to Arms*, yet it is impossible to avoid the suspicion that both Jake Barnes and Lieutenant Henry are the same character and, moreover, the only character their author can truly make. In other words, that they are Hemingway himself. It is easier to put oneself on paper than another – providing, of course, you avoid pretension. Bill Gorton's relation to Jake is much the same as Bill's to Nick in *In Our Time*, that is, each pair is one character split down the middle. I think Lady Brett Ashley also belongs to this category, being a female counterpart to Jake/Bill. But Cohn is a creation ouside Hemingway's personal sphere of conduct and belief. So is Mike. Mike is a simple achievement because he is a simple person, but Cohn was Hemingway's most successful character creation up to that date. The people of *To Have and Have Not* were too limited, or Hemingway's view of them was too limited, to stand comparison. *For Whom the Bell Tolls* breaks entirely new ground. For the first time we feel that Hemingway had studied his characters with his intelligence as well as with his senses. Doing what so many critics complained he had not done before, he proved his former rightness by partial failure. Behind every figure in this new novel lurks the author with a notebook. The characterisation is too obvious, even sluggish. The glorious carelessness of the earlier books had gone.

There may be one rival to Cohn, an unexpected one. This is the Colonel in *Across the River*, which in my view is a failure as a novel and is not even redeemed by the Colonel. I had better say at this point that although I believe moral values can and should be kept out of criticism, it is not really possible to exclude emotion. A novel read without emotional receptivity is certain to appear limp. I have sympathy with the critic who said all criticism is rationalised emotion. I have so little fellow-feeling for the Colonel that I cannot love him or feel sorry for him or think of him in any way but as a bore (probably a victim of circumstances, but still a bore). Nevertheless I do believe that he is a true creation. He may have a bit of Hemingway in him, an older Hemingway grown rather cynical, but I am in no position to say whether that is true or not. I mention the possibility simply because, if it is true, it detracts from the creativeness. Sometimes the Colonel's monologues and inner discussions with himself do not ring true, but the ring is that of a living person, not of a book-figure who hasn't been decently treated by his maker. I shall have more to say about the Colonel later.

Hemingway himself admits that it is easier to write in the first person. In an answer to one of my stupid questions he says

> When I wrote the first two novels I had not learned to write in the third person. The first person gives you great intimacy in attempting to give a complete sense of experience to the reader. It is limited however and in the third person the novelist can work in other people's heads and in other people's country. His range is greatly extended and so are his obligations. I prepared myself

for writing in the third person by the discipline of writing *Death in the Afternoon;* the short stories and especially the long short stories of 'The Short Happy Life of Francis Macomber' and 'The Snows of Kilimanjaro.' In 'The Snows of Kilimanjaro' I put in and deliberately used what could have made many novels to see how far it was possible to concentrate in a medium.

The third person requires the constant effort of projection but without its use the novelist is almost certain to move the same character through all his work. To retain the first person and yet vary the character is hardest of all. This is true of the Colonel, for although he is referred to objectively we know him chiefly through his thoughts.

'Fresh Pebbles'

Where did Hemingway learn to write in his fresh, invigorating way? Where did his words come from, those words which, in Ford Madox Ford's phrase, 'strike you, each one, as if they were pebbles fetched fresh from a brook. They live and shine, each in its place. So one of his pages has the effect of a brook-bottom into which you look down through the flowing water. The words form a tessellation, each in order beside the other.' They were not new words, like Joyce's. They were the old words used in a new way, in a new order – a new order for literature but not for the ordinary purposes of life. It is the intrusion of the language of everyday activity into the sphere of literary convention that delighted his readers. The Italian battlefields, the rout of the Greeks in Smyrna, taught the young Hemingway reality

before he had time to surrender to the shams. But
he was not alone in that. Many young men shared
the experience. Ford himself hammered one of the
cleanest prose styles of our time out of it. The influence of the Paris bars, apparently so far removed from
the normal purposes of living, helped complete this
education. The advantage of bohemianism lay in its
detachment, the opportunity it gave to dissociate oneself from the conception of society a reader gathers
from his daily newspaper. You could even work as a
newspaper man, as Hemingway did, and still stay
remote, for your money-earning self was distinct from
your true self, the one that sought for sensation as
the true aim. These men did not consider the possibility of fulfilment through vocation. They seemed
to take it for granted that one should set aside so
many hours for drudgery, perhaps as payment for the
good in life.

No one is ever the first in anything. Development is gradual, even in the age of speed. But there is
usually one person who seems to grasp a new significance before the others and exploit it. In America
Sherwood Anderson had written *Winesburg, Ohio*,
and his short, simple, direct sentences were what
Hemingway had been waiting for. Anderson was
John the Baptist. In Paris there was Gertrude Stein.
Miss Stein had the surprising faculty of being obscure
in a wonderfully simple way. But she was only obscure if you let her. If you read her work as prose,
looking for commas and grammatical constructions,
you were baffled. But if you read it as poetry, letting
the words establish their mood, the effect was at least

emotionally comprehensible. Hemingway put this technique to the service of fiction. John O'Hara writes: 'I have a theory... that all you need to know about the influence of Miss Stein on the young Ernest Hemingway is to pretend that you are, say, a Chinese who never has read English: you look at some pages of the *Autobiography of Alice B. Toklas*, then look at the superb Caporetto retreat writing in *Farewell to Arms*. You will think they were written by the same person'.[1] Personally I don't think you would but you would notice the similarities. The important thing is that Hemingway combined two traditions, perhaps three. You found in him the robustness of the best Americans (he has great admiration for Mark Twain) and the innovations of those American expatriates who had already begun to establish themselves. The third tradition is the French with its zeal and discipline. I don't think this should be over-emphasised, as much of his work, even in the early days, was distinctly ungallic. His sense of discipline is not an easy thing to convey, although I have tried to show how he combined the haphazardry of life with the control of an artist. In his very carelessness he seemed to show an instinctive sense of design.

The memory of Gertrude Stein, if not her influence, persisted. In *For Whom the Bell Tolls*, which is an object of conscious measurement compared with the earlier books, Robert Jordan discusses onions with Augustin.

---

[1] *New York Times Book Review*, 10 Sept. 1950.

'What hast thou against the onion?'

'The odour. Nothing more. Otherwise it is like the rose'.

Robert Jordan grinned at him with his mouth full.

'Like the rose', he said. 'Mighty like the rose. A rose is a rose is an onion'.

'Thy onions are affecting thy brain', Augustin said. 'Take care'.

'An onion is an onion is an onion'. Robert Jordan said cheerily and, he thought, a stone is a stein is a rock is a boulder is a pebble.

Shortly before this he had been reproaching himself for being literary. It is one of the rare references back to the days of the Lost Generation. Jordan feels a slight twinge of nostalgia for Hemingway's old days in Paris.

Scaffolds

There are two kinds of literary discipline, verbal and formal. That is why I have been diffident in my references to Hemingway's discipline. Verbal discipline, the insistence of having the right word in the right place, is his. In this he is French. But in the form of his stories and novels he is American, at times Anglo-Saxon. The most tightly organised of his books followed the least. It is part of Hemingway's literary personality that he oscillates between the possible extremes. *For Whom the Bell Tolls* is so carefully arranged and planned that the structure lies heavily on the story. We never get the feeling of life from this book that we get from *Farewell to Arms* and *Fiesta* because we are always aware of the fences by which we are enclosed. There are practically no fences

(except geographical ones) in *To Have and Have Not.*
I believe this book began its career as a short story
which was later expanded. About halfway through
an entirely new set of characters is introduced. At
first they have the appearance of extras, those accurate
little studies which were so valuable in *Fiesta* (e.g.
the English tourist, Harris) and in *Farewell to Arms*
(e.g. the Italian sergeants in the Caporetto retreat).
But these have come to stay. They have come from an
entirely different world from Harry Morgan's, a rel-
atively secure world with more money and more
education and a different way of speaking. It is the
intrusion of the Haves whom, despite the title, we
had forgotten about. The story of the Haves and
Have-Nots run side by side, rarely mingling, and
when they do it is usually by implication. Towards
the end they receive such equal prominence it is
difficult to say which group is the author's true concern, which the background. Perhaps this almost
unconnected parallelism is true of our society, yet
it makes unsatisfactory literature. An artist must
focus, must distinguish between foreground and background (unless he is an abstract painter), and Hemingway fails to do this. On reflection we may decide
that Harry Morgan is our focal point but this is not
immediately obvious, as it should be. Hemingway
may have been borrowing a technique from Dos
Passos but he does it too half-heartedly for success. In
one of the final chapters the novel seems to fly into
pieces. We are introduced to the different people
inhabiting the yachts moored to the Key West piers.
They are all biological or social degenerates, and all

are rich: quarrelsome homosexuals, a man who could not live on two hundred dollars a month and contemplated suicide, an unloved broker whose horizons were formed by speculation, a happy family whose head cannot satisfy his wife but it doesn't matter because he's made a fortune out of bottles of something everybody wants, a masturbating film actress. A wonderful picture gallery which would do well by itself in *Partisan Review* but is out of place in this novel.

The integration of *For Whom the Bell Tolls* is massive. Artistically it is a fine achievement but it has lost some of the spontaneity and poetry of the first two novels. It is not often realised how antagonistic art and poetry can be and that the fusion of the two is so rare that those who have succeeded are the truly great and can usually be counted on the fingers of one hand in any literature. In English there is of course Shakespeare, the early Wordsworth (for no writer maintains this level of excellence for a lifetime and most of those who do reach it only stay there for the course of one book or part of a book); in modern literature we can appreciate the impressive art of Ford Madox Ford and the life-giving poetry of Saroyan, but it is very rare to find a balanced combination. It is usually confined to a single chapter or poem. Reverting to *The Bell*, we may accept it as a successful work of art – but there are so many aspects that a writer has to consider or, more truly, contain through the medium of his conscious and unconscious processes. By concentrating on the structure the poetry may slip out through the back door. And then, what of the accuracy, which can again be of two kinds, internal and external?

Arturo Barea says that the reader 'may accept the book because it is a powerful work of art and implicitly believe in the inner truthfulness of Hemingway's Spain'.[1] Art in itself does not require truth or accuracy, only consistency (sometimes referred to as 'inner truth'). But literary art is a hybrid, especially when the author is relating his story to a world that is known to exist. It is natural for the reader to assume that the truth is external as well as internal. No one would even look for external truth in Kafka, for instance. In Hemingway they do.

Barea gives three instances of how the external image of *The Bell* is false, and claims that he could give others. First of all, the gypsy tart Pilar and the horse-dealer of the bullring, Pablo, would never have been accepted by a band of Castilian guerrilleros. Connected with this psychological aspect of the Spanish people is Hemingway's treatment of Spanish brutality. They would be incapable of organising slaughter like a *fiesta*, as in Pilar's story. The Spaniard only kills the thing, man or beast, that could kill him.

> Hemingway has forgotten this when he describes the collective killing of defenceless enemies in a bullring atmosphere. And yet, this is the kind of violence which the common reader would be apt to expect from Spaniards; the supreme skill of the narration makes it seem stark reality. To me, this is the worst aspect of Hemingway's fundamental mistake: he falsifies most

[1] 'Not Spain but Hemingway', Arturo Barea, *Horizon*, May 1941.

plausibly the causes and the actual form of the tragic violence of my people – not knowing that he falsifies it, because much of what he describes does exist in the Spain of the bullring, the Spain he understands and seeks to find in every Spaniard'.[1]

Secondly, Barea says Maria could not go straight to Jordan's bed, nor could she be so innocent of love and kissing as she is portrayed. And thirdly, the lyrical dialogue is too abstract. An effort is made to impress the reader with a linguistic strangeness and loftiness that is in fact non-existent. We can only regard these charges as a matter between Hemingway and the Spaniards. We are powerless to adjudicate. When W. H. Davies made tramps speak like domestic servants in a big house, we were in a position to judge and make mental allowances. In this case we have to assume that a sensitive Spaniard like Barea is probably right.

Knowing and Not Knowing

But there are many occasions on which we are able to judge Hemingway's accuracy. There are those elements of experience, for instance, which are common to humanity. To be young is probably the same for all of us emotionally. When Frederick Henry lay wounded in the hospital the lights were only turned on when a visitor came or something was being done. 'It made me feel very young to have the dark come after dusk and then remain. It was like being put to bed after early supper.' This is recognisable to all

[1] Barea, *ibid.*

of us, the helplessness of sickness. This chapter
(eleven) is a good example of Hemingway's method,
or one of his methods. He likes to sketch a scene with
a few bare yet significant strokes, follow with action
and then conversation, and then enclose the whole
with a return to the original scene. Visually it consists of broken paragraphs at beginning and end and
broken lines of conversation in between. Here we see
Henry lying in bed, then we see the arrival of the
priest and hear them discussing the war and God and
love, and finally leave him in the dark ward thinking
of the priest and his home in the Abruzzi.

Or another example of perfect observation. In
To Have and Have Not there is a vivid scene where
the drunken Veterans quarrel and drink and fight in
one of the waterfront bars. Into this pandemonium
comes the unlikely figure of Professor McWalsey.
Someone mentions a boxer who had 'the old rale'
and the Professor immediately lifts his nose, inquiring what it means. Then follows a short but intensely
serious discussion on the word and its derivation.
This is a wonderful moment of truth. Drunks, particularly uneducated drunks, love to prove their
sobriety by giving their attention to matters which
would normally be outside their scope. In every
drunken party there are islands of specious culture.

Nevertheless, you cannot assess a writer by
tabulating his moments of vision, his brilliance of
imagery, his accuracy of observation. It is possible
for a writer to be apparently deficient in all these
qualities and yet hold the imagination. (It is difficult
to state why Evelyn Waugh and Graham Greene are

good novelists for just this reason.) A good writer gives the impression of quality and the mystery lies in determining how he transmits the impression. One of the most remarkable events in the history of English literature is the fully-fledged emergence of Shelley.

> A good writer should know as near everything as possible, Hemingway says. Naturally he will not. A great enough writer seems to be born with knowledge. But he really is not; he has only been born with the ability to learn in a quicker ratio to the passage of time than other men and without conscious application, and with an intelligence to accept or reject what is already presented as knowledge.[1]

Our knowledge of communication is still slight. Intuition probably plays a much greater part in it than we think.

Hemingway goes on to say that however great the pool of knowledge available, the writer must still have a minimum of experience by whose light he can understand and assimilate it.

> If a writer of prose knows enough about what he is writing about he may omit things that he knows and the reader, if the writer is writing truly enough, will have a feeling of those things as strongly as though the writer had stated them.... A writer who omits things because he does not know them only makes hollow places in his writing.

Any writer must recognise the truth of this. This book I am writing is full of hollow places, places which I have attempted to patch over with vary-

[1] *Death in the Afternoon.*

ing success, but which will have the appearance of caverns to those who honour it with their full attention. Hemingway concludes:

> A writer who appreciates the seriousness of writing so little that he is anxious to make people see he is formally educated, cultured or well-bred is merely a popinjay. And this too remember: a serious writer is not to be confounded with a solemn writer. A serious writer may be a hawk or a buzzard or even a popinjay, but a solemn writer is always a bloody owl.

Nick Adams might easily have picked that up from Chesterton.

I only know one piece of intentionally humorous writing by Hemingway. It appeared in *The New Yorker* for February 12th 1927 under the title 'My Own Life'. It is significant that nearly all the great writers have possessed a well-developed sense of humour[1] and, moreover, have considered it a valuable part of their equipment. Most of their jokes are naturally marginal and incidental to the main theme. In this effort of Hemingway's he is as successful as anyone else. A sense of humour is either well-developed or non-existent – I doubt if there are any cases of slight sense of humour, though its mode may be quieter or subtler in some instances than in others. Rabelais is not funnier than Gogol (which would be impossible) but he may make more people laugh. Here are two examples of Hemingway's touch. Explaining how he broke with John Wilkes Booth he says, 'Why did you kill him, Booth? He'd paid for

[1] Leo Tolstoy and D. H. Lawrence are important exceptions.

his seat.' On how he broke with Gertrude Stein: 'Hemingway, why do you always come here drunk?' she asks him and he says, 'I don't know, Miss Stein, unless it's to see you.'

To Gush Or Not To Gush

Is there ever a need for pretentious writing? Hemingway, of all people, says there is and in this point alone one must succumb to a feeling of admiration for his honesty or what he calls seriousness. Suppose you are writing for someone who isn't even on speaking terms with your subject? Will a bare statement convey your feeling? There must, says Hemingway, be that initial sympathy or at least a sharing of experience. If not the effect on the reader may be equivalent to that of a geometrical proposition. (This could explain why one set of people rave about a writer's emotional punch and another set complain about his coldness.) Here is Hemingway's example:

> ... sometimes standing absolutely straight with his feet still, planted as though he were a tree, with the arrogance and grace that gypsies have and of which all other arrogance and grace seems an imitation, moves the cape spread full as the pulling jib of a yacht before the bull's muzzle so slowly that the art of bullfighting, which is only kept from being one of the major arts because it is impermanent, in the arrogant slowness of his veronicas becomes, for the seeming minutes that they endure, permanent. That is the worst sort of flowery writing, but it is necessary to try to give the feeling, and to someone who has never seen it a simple statement of the method does not convey the feeling. Any-

one who has seen bull fights can skip such flowerish-
ness and read the facts which are much more difficult
to isolate and state.[1]

The popular opinion is, then, that Hemingway
refuses to gush and romanticise. It is his great
strength. He himself says it is occasionally necessary
and gives an instance. But what seems almost sacrilege
occurs when up pops a critic and accuses Hemingway
of gushing unconsciously! It is very good for the
soul to be shown up in this way and I think Mr.
Eastman scores a palpable hit. He distinguishes between the bull that gets winded quickly and stands
with its tongue hanging out and the bull that gets
tired in the muscles before it gets winded. The latter
bull's tongue stays in its mouth.

> This plain fact, which would be obvious to anybody
> without smoke in his eyes, is romanticised by Heming-
> way to mean that some bulls are so 'brave' that they
> will never let their tongues out, but hold their mouths
> 'tight shut to keep the blood in' even after they are
> stabbed to death and until they drop. This is not
> juvenile romanticism, it is child's fairy-story writing.[2]

Eastman is so pleased with himself that he spoils an
excellent point by making that unreal distinction
between juvenile romanticism and fairy-story writing.

Still, this is not the real Hemingway. The real
Hemingway contrives a flatness of tone that excludes
emotion, gush, romanticising and fantasy. His

[1] *Death in the Afternoon.*
[2] 'Bull in the Afternoon', *Ernest Hemingway: the Man
and his Work,* ed. McCaffery.

methods are simple. The effect is made by his homely words but the most effective device comes from his use of the conjunction 'and'. Time after time it is used when a conventional writer would have used 'but' and instead of the subsequent phrase conveying surprise or horror or discontent it is reduced to acceptance. Hemingway must have been one of the first to have used this now over-familiar device. Lesser writers have put it to a cheap and automatic use. Here is a genuine usage by Hemingway. It occurs after Macomber, having disgraced himself before his wife, has shot the buffalo. 'The car was parallel to the patch of bush. Macomber, Wilson and the gun-bearer got down. Macomber, looking back, saw his wife, with the rifle by her side, looking at him, looking at him. He waved to her and she did not wave back.' It is an effective device when used with restraint as here. In the first few paragraphs of *Farewell to Arms* Hemingway 'used the word "and" consciously over and over the way Mr. Johann Sebastian Bach used a note in music when he was emitting counterpoint'.[1] The effect is good here too because it is a passage of straight description. It is when it is used insistently for the evocation of surprise that it wearies the reader.

The flat unadorned statement can be used for another effect than emotional inhibition and description though it occurs much less frequently. This is irony. If you describe really outrageous events as though they happen daily in your back yard you get

[1] Lillian Ross quoting Hemingway in *The New Yorker* Profile.

a critical impact which Woe Woe and Cry Havoc
do not impart. Like this: 'The Greeks were nice
chaps too. When they evacuated they had all their
baggage animals they couldn't take off with them so
they just broke their forelegs and dumped them into
the shallow water. All those mules with their forelegs
broken pushed over into the shallow water. It was all
a pleasant business. My word, yes, a most pleasant
business'.[1] I don't think this kind of attack is to be
found outside the stories.

Some readers have referred to the sense of
embarrassment they feel in front of Hemingway's
nakedness. Spender says he has always been disappointed by Hemingway's stories because 'he has
confined himself to presenting the reader with a situation, violent, horrible or beautiful, as a child might
come up and leave a stone, an insect or a flower in
your hand'.[2] Hemingway's attempt to present a philosophy of life, he added, was embarrassing. On the
one hand he dislikes the absence of comment, on the
other he is uncomfortable when it is present. This is
a good instance of how there are wings to criticism,
as there are to politics, and how you can find them
co-existing in the same person. In the Preface to *The
First Forty-Nine* (the collected short stories), published in 1939, Hemingway adopts a button-holing
approach, with traces of a spurious simplicity and
humility which we do not find in the stories themselves. After listing some good places to work in he
writes: 'Some other places were not so good, but

[1] 'On the Quai at Smyrna'.
[2] 'Books and the War', *Penguin New Writing* No. 5.

maybe we were not so good when we were in them.'
But I do not take this flaccidity too seriously. It is
probably the product of Hemingway's having to write
something he didn't want to write. 'And would you
let us have a few words by way of introduction, Mr.
Hemingway?' Again, running all through *For Whom
the Bell Tolls* there is a touch of portentousness,
accentuated by the unfailing use of Robert Jordan's
full name, making him distant, almost some kind of
demigod set apart from the rest of the characters
and us.

The Wow and the Moral

Hemingway is a highly conscious writer, by
which I mean he thinks about his medium. He has
managed to put the results of some of his thinking
into his book on bullfights, as we have already seen,
sometimes in a somewhat glancing, tangential way.
In this book he records conversations with an imagin-
ary old lady. Having listened to one of his slice-of-
life stories she says: 'And is that all of the story? Is
there not to be what we called in my youth a wow
at the end?'

'Ah, madame, it is years since I added the wow
to the end of the story.'

There is, in fact, at least one example of a trick
O. Henry ending in his work. This is in the story 'A
Canary for One'.[1] It is a friendly kind of story, with
a deaf American lady on a train reminiscing about
her daughter who had had the misfortune to fall in
love with a Swiss. She repeated several times, 'Ameri-

[1] From *Men Without Women*.

cans make the best husbands.' There is an air of general agreement. It seems impossible that Americans should make anything but the best husbands. The American who is telling the story and his wife talk to the old lady about her daughter and her clothes-buying. At the end of the journey they say goodbye. The last sentence says: 'We were returning to Paris to set up separate residences.'

When all these points have been taken into consideration, Hemingway's chief strength remain in his directness of approach. Like Saroyan, he has the rare distinction of either writing his own work or, at worst, when harried and unnerved by malice, a parody of it. There is none of the immaculate tailoring, done to the measure of some fashionable editor or publisher, that is acclaimed with such whoops of joy by reviewers in the weekly papers. Perhaps Hemingway had the advantage of being able to write outside his own shadow. It seems to be increasingly difficult these days for a young writer to think of himself as a person. He is always After the Lost Generation or a Converted Catholic or a Neo-Kafkan. As I have tried to show, Hemingway had his influences but he stood aside from them. (I will develop this point in the next chapter.) The best thing to do with an influence is to fly from it like a burglar, clutching the silver. When he put in a manuscript of stories his belief that *The Enormous Room* was the greatest book he had ever read, Gertrude Stein said to him, 'Hemingway, remarks are not literature'.[1] After that Hemingway went on making

[1] *The Autobiography of Alice B. Toklas.*

remarks but he made sure they came from the mouths of his characters.

There are two ways of making a comment, moralist and descriptive. Gertrude Stein probably did more than anyone to smother the tiny moralist that might have peeped through, the one that wanted to admire E. E. Cummings in public. The other type, which is much more common and much less objectionable, was purged by Hemingway himself. There were a few early examples, e.g.

> 'He claims he's never taken a drink in his life', Nick said, as though announcing a scientific fact.[1]

Later Hemingway wouldn't have told us how he said it. He would have left it to our imagination. If we couldn't see for ourselves that he said it as a scientific fact, then there would not be much point in telling us, for we would be hopelessly outside the story. But every method has its limitation, as Hemingway himself has admitted. Some ideas or emotional values cannot be imparted by purely objective description. For instance, Hemingway writes: 'This honour thing is not some fantasy that I am trying to inflict on you in the way writers on the peninsula give out their theories on its people. I swear it is true.'[2] He is reduced to putting his hand on his heart. It might be objected that he could have told us convincingly in fiction and in this book he is not writing fiction, but the fact remains that there are occasions when you must believe the author because you have been

[1] 'The Three-Day Blow', *In Our Time*.
[2] *Death in the Afternoon*.

brought face to face with him and there is no other
evidence. Literary criticism, or a large part of it,
resolves itself into knowing whom to believe and
whom not to believe – and that is not a logical process
at all.

The Entry of Hate

When hatred or dislike get the better of him
Hemingway's accuracy suffers. They are held on a
tight rein until *To Have and Have Not* and then they
get another airing in *Across the River*. It is inevitable
that he should feel contempt for mere desk-squatters.
His method will not allow him to make a full-blooded
attack, except through the mouth of one of his characters. But there is another way which it can be
done and that is by caricature. We get the first Hemingway caricature in *To Have and Have Not*. The
self-important bureaucrat and administrator is, from
the point of view of an artist and man of action, a
ridiculous person. But such men are too cunning and
also too intelligent to wear their ridicule like a badge.
When Frederick Harrison and his secretary are trying
to take Harry Morgan they talk like parodies of
themselves.

> 'You're really capturing him single-handed', said
> the secretary admiringly.
> 'And unarmed too', said Frederick Harrison.
> 'With no G-men nonsense', said the secretary.

Undoubtedly Frederick Harrison and his secretary feel this way. There is to little fantasy in their
own lives they do not pass over a gift like this. But

they do not speak their thoughts for they retain a strong sense of reality.

In another passage Hemingway describes a meeting in a bar between the Laughtons and the Gordons. It is good enough observation, accurately enough presented, but it doesn't belong to the novel we started reading. Once again we feel that Hemingway's bitterness against those of his own profession who parade their erudition and education is getting the better of his sense of balance. We hear a young man referring to a woman as a social phenomenon and telling his companions that a writer 'can't restrict his experience to conform to bourgeois standards' – phrases that Hemingway feels should not be taken out of lecture rooms. The theme is true enough but it is inessential. It comes from that part of Hemingway that tilted at Aldous Huxley and perhaps at T.S. Eliot in *Death in the Afternoon*.

In *Across the River* there is a tirade from the Colonel against his journalist wife. This is of course permissible and again I must stress the critic's obligation of refraining from telling the novelist what he should write and how he should write it. The reason I mention this and other examples of vituperation is because they were absent from the early novels. It is as though an emotional nerve had been jarred during the intervening period. If these are the new tricks the old ones have become clichés. Compared with *Fiesta* this novel lacks spontaneity, is sluggish and dull. Perhaps it is a matter of time. Perhaps we should not expect the same vitality from a man of fifty that we had from one of thirty. It is not even easy to

feel that Hemingway himself was interested in the
Colonel. It reads like an interim novel in which he
cleanses himself of the dross he has accumulated.
Perhaps the return to Italy created unmanageable
comparisons and revived the power of his early
war-wound. Hemingway himself (not the Colonel)
writes phrases that he would once have condemned as
romantic gush. 'He whispered this last so low that it
was inaudible to anyone who did not love you.' That
is not a man in love but a man trying hard to remember love. (Love, like bullfighting, is not a major art
because it is impermanent.) There is a retreat from
the concrete Hemingway forced us to feel to abstractions he begs us to sense.

> She kissed him kind, and hard, and desperately, and
> the Colonel could not think about any fights or any
> picturesque or strange incidents. He only thought of
> her and how she felt and how close life comes to death
> when there is ecstasy. And what the hell is ecstasy and
> what's ecstasy's rank and serial number? And how does
> her black sweater feel? And who made all her smooth-
> ness and delight and the strange pride and sacrifice
> and wisdom of a child? Yes, ecstasy is what you might
> have had and instead you draw sleep's other brother.

The black sweater links us with the past. The
inquiry after ecstasy's rank and serial number hints
at a doubt in Hemingway's mind: *is* there such a
thing as ecstasy? have I ever touched it or seen its
outline or taken it with me to Big Two-Hearted
River?

93

CHAPTER V

THE CHAMPION

IT was the style that won the disciples but the disciples very soon discovered that the style belonged to a remarkable man. It is not often that a literary leader is capable of becoming a hero or leader of men. He is rarely a man of action for there is rarely sufficient energy in the one frame to encompass both rôles. But Hemingway is an exception. If he had never been a writer his great strength, his sporting skill and his flair for an adventurous situation would still have enabled him to make his mark in a chaotic society for which he seems to have been specially designed. To begin with, he is a big man with the kind of body than can be used for busting through tough spots. 'His body is enormous and oddly proportioned. Most of his 215-odd pounds are in his upper torso and extremities...... His legs are thin to the point of being delicate, but his barrel chest, shoulders and arms are huge. So are his hands; shaking hands with Hemingway is a good deal like bumping into a door.'[1] A boxer named Harry Sylvester with whom Hemingway used to spar told John McCaffery that he was the strongest man that he had ever known. He used to box at 198 pounds. He has become known as a fisherman, not of small fry but of giant marlin and tuna. (His first weighed 468 pounds and he brought it to gaff in 65 minutes without using a harness.) He had a name for fighting and

[1] Sam Boal, 'I Tell You True', *Park East*, January 1951.

boating his fish fast before the sharks had time to mutilate them. With the strength goes endurance. When he took *For Whom the Bell Tolls* to the printer there were still revisions to be made. He rented a drawing room on the train from Miami to New York and worked straight through at a temperature of 128, the air-conditioning system being out of order. When he received the galley proofs he worked on them in his hotel for 96 hours without leaving the room. Damon Runyon said of him, 'Few men can stand the strain of relaxing with him over an extended period.'

Those who know him insist that the stories about him are true. There is a real background to the legend. There are many stories of his courage, particularly during the last war when he roamed the Western Theatre in his own style. One example will suffice, told by John Groth.

> On the way back to the farmhouse we stopped at a regimental command post. The colonel was briefing his officers at dinner. With more men and material coming up, the outlook was good. There was warm food; they had been on K rations. It was pleasant inside. Pictures..... had been brought by Hemingway, and they were being passed around when an explosion batted through the window, breaking it, and cutting loose the lamp from the ceiling. Eighty-eights were coming in. When candles were lighted we were all – officers and correspondent – on the floor, making ourselves small and groping for helmets. All, that is, except one: Hemingway was still seated at the table, his broad back to the window, helmetless, eating.[1]

[1] 'A Note on Ernest Hemingway', *Ernest Hemingway: the Man and his Work*, ed. McCaffery.

It is impossible to live the kind of life that Hemingway has lived (war, game hunting, poking his nose into dangerous corners) and come out unscarred. He is in fact scarred from head to foot. Courage, either moral or physical, is one of the chief things he demands from his friends. They are an assorted set, including wealthy sportsmen, generals, priests, prize-fighters, jockeys, matadors, movie stars and ex-convicts. They are all men and women who have taken risks and their mortality rate is high.

He lives big too. At his Spanish-style farmhouse, Finca Vigia, everything is on a patriarchal scale, Hemingway surrounded by family, friends and retainers. Fifteen acres with gardens, tennis court and swimming pool, and a white tower with his study at the top. The living room is sixty feet long and is lined with heads of beasts we met in *Green Hills of Africa*. The Chinese cook never knows how many for dinner. Two houseboys, two or three gardeners, a chauffeur for the two cars and station wagon, an engineer for the fishing boat. Cats vary in number from about twenty to fifty. He picks up people, stewards, tramps or film stars, who stay with him indefinitely. At the back of all this is a very large income.

The rough, tough, fighting literary man is a character that has immense appeal for some people. For others it is a contradiction in terms. From both angles the story gets out of hand. Probably the most notorious even in Hemingway's life was not the publication of *Fiesta* but his fight with Max Eastman. One set of people say, You see, our hero can do the

things he writes about; another set says scornfully,
And this is supposed to be a great writer! The story
has been degraded to a boasting match about who
had the most hairs on his chest. It has become known
as The Fight and it flourishes on guesswork. Probably
the only people who really knew what happened were
Hemingway, Eastman and Max Perkins, their publisher, and only Perkins had an unprejudiced view of
things, and he's dead now. What more could the
legend-mongers want? Hemingway himself is disgusted by the furore resulting from this piece of
emotion-in-action. He writes in a letter: '. . . a
book of mine is judged by some people on a basis
of criticism which seems to depend on whether I hit
some man in a place like the Stork Club (after being
goaded into it) than on the merits or demerits of
the book.' The parenthesis is such a human last
word.

One result of Hemingway's very real love of the
open-air and sporting life is his frequent analogy
between life and sport. Although he is insistent on
his seriousness with regard to writing it is impossible
to feel that he feels the same about life itself. We are
part of life, pitched into it whether we like it or not,
and it is useless to complain or pretend that our
views on the subject are going to produce much of a
repercussion on the question of comingness and
goingness. Life is the framework which we accept.
Our energies must be directed towards the segments
of life, not towards its wholeness. It is therefore perfectly rational to torture oneself about writing or
endanger oneself in sport and at the same time remain

quite unmoved by the religious purpose or meta-
physical desing of the whole of which they are parts.
For Hemingway it is only possible to know life
through some such activity as writing or sport. In
short, life becomes an abstraction or something that
is too large for the individual to grasp. One can write
and be a writer, shoot game or box and be a sportsman, and in this way be part of the greater thing, life,
up to the hilt. But it's no good trying to get round
the scabbard, trying to bracket the unknown with
arms trained for shooting or loving or drinking.
Sometimes, in one of his expansive moods (more frequent in his later writings) Hemingway writes about
'life' but nearly always as a reflection of sport, the
thing he knows and is good at. The few people who
have been allowed to interview him agree on this. For
instance, according to Harvey Breit he said, 'Life is
the greatest left-hooker so far, although many say it
was Charley White of Chicago.'[1] This kind of moralising is applied to anything that interests him. Is he a
sectional or national writer? No, a good writer is just
a writer. 'That's the hard league to play in. The ball
is standard, the ball parks vary somewhat, but they
are all good. There are no bad bounces. Alibis don't
count. Go out and do your stuff.'[2] Critics? 'They are
like those people who go to ball games and can't tell
the players without a score card. I am not worried
about what anybody I do not like might do. What
the hell! If they can do you harm, let them do it.

[1] 'Talk with Mr. Hemingway', *New York Times*, 17 Sept.
[2] Quoted by Malcolm Cowley, 'A Portrait of Mr. Papa',
from *Ernest Hemingway*, ed. J. McCaffery.

It is like being a third baseman and protesting because they hit line drives to you.'[1]

It is amusing to think that English writers were persuaded to drop the sporting metaphor over a generation ago. Of course, they did it with enormous pomposity, capitalising the Great Game of Life and always referring to the Aweful Umpire who controlled the game sternly and mercilessly. The Great Game had a tendency to resemble cricket, which handicapped the lesser breeds. Hemingway has a tendency to find the key in baseball, thus avenging one section of the human race on another. I don't know whether he objects to the publicity that has been given to his sporting analogy, which may be just a private convenience which has crept from his thought into his conversation and should never be treated as a public philosophy. I do know that he objects to the 'sort of half choctaw dialect' in which he is alleged to give it expression. But perhaps the analogy is a universal one, not limited to English academicians and American tough guys. In Osbert Sitwell's *Great Morning* a dying gamekeeper says to the doctor, 'You've got t'old cock bird down, Doctor, but I don't know whether you're going to bag him now or not.'

It is time we had a look at where this man came from. There was nothing remarkable about his family background. There were no Negro giants behind him, as with Alexandre Dumas, nor was he the illegitimate son of a dictator. He was born in 1898 in Oak Park, a Chicago suburb and the middle-class

[1] Quoted by Lillian Ross, Profile, *The New Yorker*.

capital of the world. His father was a doctor who taught Ernest to hunt and fish, chiefly when on holiday in Michigan. (We meet him or someone like him in the stories of *In Our Time*.) His mother was a music-lover and the Hemingways used to invite audiences to their large music room to hear her sing. His parents gave him a fishing rod, shotgun and cello. He scamped the cello for fishing. At fourteen Ernest took boxing lessons and had his nose broken by Young A'Hearn, but he kept going, despite damage to his eye. He was a good footballer but missed important games through injury. He had the inner urge to excel at everything. He edited the school weekly and wrote stories for the school quarterly. He belonged to the debating club, the Hanna Club (lectures by prominent citizens), the Boys' Rifle Club, played in the school orchestra, was in the swimming team, managed the track team, wrote the class prophecy. He wasn't happy at school and twice ran away from home. He didn't go to dances until his last year. His classmates say he was a lonely boy, despite his wide activities, and they made him the butt of their jokes. This may be a parallel to the contemporary practice of nonentity journalists in trying to make a fool out of him. Some people don't like too high a standard of achievement to be set against their own failures.

Then the War, enlistment in an Italian ambulance unit, the leg wound that meant so much to him. (The first of the many scars, but a multiple one.) Another complete break, with the middle-western boy now living the bohemian life in Paris 1921. We have a quick sketch of Hemingway by Ford Madox Ford, advancing with 'rather the aspect of an Eton-Oxford, huskyish young captain of a midland regiment of His Britannic Majesty... balancing on the point of his toes, feinting at my head with hands as large as hams, and relating sinister stories of Paris landlords'. At first Hemingway was a journalist, that is to say, he had not yet learnt to distinguish between journalism and writing. It was Gertrude Stein who saw the spark and advised him to concentrate on *writing*. At first Gertrude preferred his poems to his prose. She was always grateful to him, despite differences of opinion, because he was the first of the young men to come knocking at her door, and because he was instrumental in getting 'really the beginning of modern writing' *(The Making of Americans)* published.

But Gertrude Stein had not been the first, except indirectly. In 1919 Hemingway had returned from Italy and had taken a job as editor of a house-organ for the Cooperative Society of America. It was then that he met Sherwood Anderson. Gertrude Stein must come first in any listing of Hemingway's influences, not only because hers was the most fruitful one but also because Anderson had learnt many of his tricks from her. Anderson was first in time, Stein in importance.

> Since Hemingway was only twenty-one and just seized with the passion to be a writer, it was only natural that he should seek to pattern his career after Anderson. He saw in the older man a spirit that resembled his in many ways, the same turning away from organised

education, the same revolt against bourgeois standards of security, the same interest in sports and the life of simple unsophisticated people. In regard to style he sensed that Anderson had turned back to a direct simplicity of language that would best fit his own nature.[1]

But Hemingway had the healthy faculty of outgrowing his influences. By 1926 and *The Torrents of Spring* he was criticising the older man for work that he felt was not up to standard.

I am referring here to his relationships with the two writers to whom he probably owed most rather than in the previous chapter because Hemingway was, by hard work and hard, instinctive criticism, establishing his position as literary idol. During the 'twenties this robust man with the robust style was compelling the younger writers, both his contemporaries and those who came after, to look to him for a lead. By the 'thirties he was one of the four writers who, according to John Lehmann, offered positive foundations for those who wished to become writers. The others were E. M. Forster, D. H. Lawrence and Wilfred Owen.[2] It is not easy to agree with the choice of this quadrumvirate: Forster is questionable and there are others who might be admitted. But there is no doubt that Hemingway should be one of them. *Fiesta, Farewell to Arms* and the short stories had settled that. The position Hemingway holds now was fought for in the 'twenties and was consolidated by *For Whom the Bell Tolls*, which has the air of having

[1] James Schevill, *Sherwood Anderson: His Life and Work*.
[2] *New Writing in Europe*.

been written by an elder statesman. The legend-making belongs largely to the later period. Arthur Koestler once told the Americans, 'Don't underestimate your Hemingway. It is banal, but he is still the greatest living writer.' Even Ehrenburg has capitulated: 'the best writer in the world today is not a Russian at all.' Even Hemingway's wife agrees. 'Who is the greatest writer in America?' asked the Austrian in *Green Hills of Africa*. 'My husband', she said.

One gets the feeling with Hemingway that he made up his mind very early to become top writer and made everything else subservient to it. There must have been cases in which a writer was determined to become a good writer, but the competitive spirit that flows from Hemingway anecdotes is something new. Whatever he does, he wishes to do it best. Some people, including writers like Shaw, hold the competitive spirit in such horror that this trait tends to destroy their appreciation of Hemingway's work. I doubt if it is any more important or vicious than the desire to win a fight or football match. Perhaps it is perverse to bring literature into the arena but we have already seen how the sectors of life in which he participates are always envisaged by Hemingway in sporting terms. (Nor did he invent the Nobel and Pulitzer Prizes, which are an invitation to competitiveness.) Even in those sports where there is not normally the competitive element Hemingway manages to inject it. When he went game-hunting it was imperative that he should have the best bag.

'I love it', I said, 'but I don't want that guy to beat

me. Pop, he's got the best buff, the best rhino, the best water-buck –'.

'You beat him on oryx', Pop said.

'What's an oryx?'

'He'll look damned handsome when you get him home'.

'I'm just kidding'.

'You beat him on impalla, on eland. You've got a firstrate bushbuck. Your leopard's as good as his'.[1]

If sport is a mirror of life it is also a mirror of any other activity in life, such as writing. Today he says, 'I'm modest. I just want to be Champion.' Some say he is. Judgment is difficult. Perhaps it is this difficulty, this constant absence of certainty, that causes artists to fly off the handle so easily. Their work is always 'in progress', there is no finality to it, except with the few like Hardy or Forster who pull down the shutters with a deliberate bang. But Hemingway can probably get far more satisfaction out of knowing that he holds the world's championship for tuna than out of hoping he is World Literary Champ.

The chorus of approval reaches its peak with John O'Hara who calls Hemingway 'the outstanding author since the death of Shakespeare'.[2] Without considering that, we may at least consider his status as a literary personality, owing less to his actual written work than to the legend that has accrued. I will refer to the legend in detail later. Here and now I want to consider it chiefly as something that gets in the way of true appraisal. Hemingway belongs to those few spirits like Trelawney, Wilde, Shaw and Byron whose

[1] *Green Hills of Africa.*

[2] *The New York Times Book Review*, 10 Sept. 1950.

personal myths have overshadowed their work. A public discussion of Hemingway's work is impossible; unless it is confined to the privacy of the study we are certain to be disturbed by the intrusion of the Big Game Hunter and War Correspondent. The spread of the legend, resulting in an expanding reputation among people who never read his books, really dated from the Spanish War and came to full status during the World War. (There had been an earlier, Lost Generation legend but it was limited and by now submerged. The new one was spread by films and magazines.) Hemingway made many friends in Spain and the good feeling spread. Arturo Barea describes him at the time:

> big and lumbering, with the look of a worried boy on his round face, diffident and yet consciously using his diffidence as an attraction, a good fellow to drink with, fond of dirty jokes 'pour épater l'Espagnol', questioning, sceptical and intelligent in his curiosity, skilfully stressing his political ignorance, easy and friendly, yet remote and somewhat sad.[1]

One reason Hemingway found it easy to communicate his personality was because he rarely chose the company of intellectuals. In Spain he mixed with the soldiers while others talked the sun down with political speculation. This is in keeping with his normal mode of expression. He does not chew the cud of theory like the intellectual but gets his teeth into everyday details as the soldier is compelled to. When asked to say something about contemporary themes,

[1] 'Not Spain but Hemingway', *Horizon*, May 1941.

he replied: 'The themes have always been love, lack of it, death and its occasional temporary avoidance which we describe as life, the immortality or lack of immortality of the soul, money, honor and politics.'[1] This is as far as he is likely to go in abstraction. It is much closer to the myth-seeking mind of ordinary man than the analyses which probe into matters of original sin, guilt complex and mother fixation. They formed the raw material of older myths which have lost their overt attraction. The secret of Hemingway's power is probably his unashamed and much publicised determination to enjoy himself, which is exactly what most people want to do, but few have sufficient confidence to say it openly. He is not a writer who announces a search for the Holy Grail. The ordinary man is doubtful of its value. He can see that Hemingway's 'dammed good life' would be damned good for him too, and, so Hemingway earns his admiration.

A lot of Hemingway's conversation, his own and his characters', and also his descriptive and narrative prose, has a clumsy feel to it. It is like a man groping for the most effective expression. He can at times talk fluently and coherently, especially about his craft, but he never loses the common-man touch. 'Like so many Americans, he has an immense gift of the gab, combined with a distrust of the power of all coherent language to express truth, an unnerving fear that logical thought and speech, may, after all, be meaningless fripperies.'[2] He probably does think that

[1] Harvey Breit, *The New York Times*, 17 Sept. 1950.
[2] Profile, *The Observer*, 10 Sept. 1950.

much of what passed for literature, no matter how coherent it might appear, was a meaningless frippery. The mind slides over the shiny surface of academic clichés.

Sam Boal has even tried to pass Hemingway off as a great conversationalist. In evidence he gives the rather surprising information that in one ten-minute conversation Hemingway 'brought up' eight subjects, including the origin of Thanksgiving, Tintoretto and How To Cook A Grouse. It may be rather English of me to say so but I doubt if this is most people's idea of conversation; the view that it is gives us an interesting glimpse of his personality and its power over those who know him. We are acquainted with those people whose slightest utterance is treasured by disciples and later published as revelation. In Hemingway's case we see that anything he does or says is liable to be dubbed 'great'. This reveals better than any action of his own the extent to which he has become a myth-hero. For the record, his talk is said to be mountainous in wisdom, steady in output and reminiscent in content. I can accept the last two. A close study of his writing leaves me unable to accept the first. He is a fine chronicler but I doubt if he approaches wisdom. I also doubt that he believes it of himself. But he has fans who are liable to enthrone him as King of Anything.

The distinguishing feature of his style, which we are told is true also of his conversation (and this is supported by examples given by journalists whom I have to take on trust), apart from its grittiness, lies in the absence of adjectives. Boal says he not only spares the adjective but omits the article: 'Man needs food. Where is waiter?' One day it may become difficult to accept the fact that Hemingway and Sir Osbert Sitwell were contemporaries. (Hemingway was born in 1899, Sitwell in 1892.) They went to war at about the same time and they have shared a world. Yet while Hemingway spits out his words, races through life and rarely pauses for reflection, Sitwell lingers over every syllable, every memory and sensation, and is reluctant to pass to the next for fear some juice should remain unsqueezed. Such contrasts reveal Hemingway more effectively than any close appreciation.

Concentrating on the man it is easy to lose the writer, which would be a pity, especially as it is the writer we are trying to pin down. So far I have referred to Hemingway's childhood and youth, his great strength, his competitive spirit, his addiction to sport, his courage, the people who influenced him, the type of friend he likes, the growth of the Hemingway legend, his conversational style. But how do all these things make a complete man and how are they transmuted into the writing? Hemingway's friend, novelist John O'Hara, tries to give the answer. O'Hara, like Hemingway, is an entirely creative and reproductive writer – that is to say, his mind has no traces of the analytical faculty. When a writer of this type is asked for an opinion he usually gives a rather chaotic, impressionist sprawl which one flounders in like a swamp. And yet I normally find these sprawls more rewarding, certainly more spirited and intuitive than the measured pace of the trained critic, pigeonholing everything into prearranged categories and rejecting those pieces that won't fit the patent puzzle. And, of course, O'Hara is a novelist, which means he knows how a novelist goes to work. All this by way of justification for a long quote but one that knits up Ernest Hemingway of Oak Park and Finca Vigia with the author of *Fiesta* and *Across the River*.

> But what Hemingway has – and Steinbeck has it too – is pre-paper discipline. It means, first of all, point of view. A great many non-writers have it without having to reveal it; but with an author it is not only revealing; it is often exposing. A possibly over-simplified definition of point-of view would be "feeling and preference" and, in an author's case, the expression of an attitude. It is in the manner and method of the expression of the attitude that writers vary, and before that, the pre-paper discipline – the thinking, the self-editing – gets its test.
>
> An author may seem to lead a ruggedly simple life, but the fact that he is an author makes him not a simple individual. The personality therefore requires enormous discipline in putting the uncomplicated thinking down on paper. The ostensibly simple lives led by men like Hemingway and Steinbeck tell practically nothing about the personalities, although the writing is simple too. The ostensibly simple life led by William Faulkner tells nothing about him either, for the writing comes out plain but complicated, with so little change in the process between first thoughts and final printed page that Faulkner, while a genius, may not be an artist. It makes damn small difference to him or to me.[1]

[1] *The New York Times Book Review*, 10 Sept. 1950.

It is best not to over-comment on this, as it speaks for itself. I merely wish to draw attention to three points which concern us in the liaison I am trying to make. First, 'feeling and preference', arising out of biological factors (practically unknown) and experience, to which I have alluded in some detail. Second, 'pre-paper discipline', getting the unwieldy 'point of view' into manageable shape. Thirdly, the complicated personality disciplining its thought and observation into an acceptably simplified expression. This does not link man and writer completely for only complete knowledge of both would make it possible. But we have noted the feeling and preference for sport and competition, seen it become manageable and organisable in, say, *To Have and Have Not* and watched the complicated personality finding an acceptable expression in *For Whom the Bell Tolls*.

The writer must purify himself where the man cannot. A man's life is constant repetition but a writer's work must avoid this above all else. Writing becomes progressively more difficult. The first books are excavations of untapped resources; later comes refinement and search at deeper levels. 'Should I repeat myself? I don't think so. You have to repeat yourself again and again as a man but you should not do so as a writer.'[1] There has naturally been overlapping in his work on the whole each novel has taken us to new ground.

[1] Hemingway, quoted by Harvey Breit, *The New York Times*, 17 Sept. 1950.

By Way of Epilogue

(a) There is an opposition to the rough portrait I have tried to make. It is a dual one and half of it, the uninformed and probably envious, is not worth bothering about. It merely rates Hemingway as a loud-mouthed boaster, forgetting that a *mere* loud-mouthed boaster could not produce *Fiesta, Farewell to Arms,* the night scene in *To Have and Have Not,* Pilar's story in *For Whom the Bell Tolls,* the critical acuteness of *Death in the Afternoon.* But Gertrude Stein is a different matter. When she got together with Sherwood Anderson they discussed this phenomenon they had helped to produce. They agreed that Hemingway was yellow, that he imitated well without understanding, that he smelt of museums and was easily tired. These are charges that are so far removed from the picture I get from his work and his other friends I confess that I cannot assimilate them. That is why I separate them — they may be cream or they may be dregs. Someone will taste them in 200 years' time and get to know the truth. But it is easier to see what Gertrude was getting at when she told him he was ninety percent Rotarian. 'Can't you, he said, make it eighty percent? No, she said regretfully, I can't.'[1] Hemingway likes many of the things Rotarians value, even if he couldn't settle down to sell shares or manage a hardware store. He could make a damn good speech at a Rotary dinner. No Rotar-

[1] *The Autobiography of Alice Toklas.*

ian would reject the opportunity to shoot Big Game and some of them became Generals in times of stress. Hemingway is partial to Generals.

As for Sherwood, he regretfully came to the conclusion that Hemingway was too self-centred. They tried to settle it over a drink but failed. Hemingway tended to identify himself with American literature, which he was determined to save.

(b) On the subject of critics Hemingway is sometimes explosive. He believes, quite rightly, that they are often not interested in the work under review. Instead they prefer to pass judgment on the writer's private life or an idea which he doesn't hold but which they think he holds or ought to hold. The activity of critics can be dangerous, erosive like wind and rain. It is not wise for a writer to read the critics. They will confuse him. They will fill his head with notions that are better withheld. All this is something quite apart from the bitterness that is the professional malady of critics, although they are often skilled enough to clothe their prejudice in weighty phrases of seeming objectivity. Hemingway's acuteness is brought to its finest pitch when he considers these natural enemies. (He must feel like a kudu with himself to windward.) Everyone knows that praise is not always helpful to the writer. (If anyone praises this book I shall be extremely annoyed.) Hemingway can see the implication.

If they believe the critics when they say they are great

then they must believe them when they say they are rotten and they lose confidence. At present we have two good writers who cannot write because they have lost confidence through reading critics. If they wrote, sometimes it would be good and sometimes not so good and sometimes it would be quite bad, but the good would get out. But they have read the critics and they must write masterpieces. They weren't masterpieces, of course. They were just quite good books. So now they cannot write at all. The critics have made them impotent.[1]

Should a writer believe he is good or not? If he doubts his goodness he will write without confidence and his work will stumble. If he doubts his badness his work will be superficial and it will bore. Critics and editors are always demanding excellence. Editors have told me that they insist on excellence in all the work they print and they actually believed they achieved it, though their faith was refuted weekly when their organs appeared on the news stands. Some would reject *David Copperfield* because it contains self-pity, *The Daring Young Man on the Flying Trapeze* for its sentimentality, *The Tropic of Cancer* for its obscenity, *The Memoirs of a Midget* for its whimsicality. If your eyes are constantly wide for excellence you won't see it. There's too much grit flying about. Excellence comes in by the back door and is frequently not recognised, not for a hundred years anyway. What about Melville? In a letter Hemingway insisted on the difficulty of understanding that exists between the

[1] *Green Hills of Africa.*

113

writer and even the best critics. Any man is liable
to be prejudiced about his own life since he knows
things about it that the most sympathetic critic
could not possibly understand because he lacks
the context of 24 hours a day for 50 years. Critics
have to examine the skin and do their best to
deduce the skeleton and gastric juices. After suffering from the attention of people who wanted
to put the True Hemingway on paper for people
to rub their hands over, he had a fit of revulsion
and for twelve years refused to give a newspaper
interview. He say he has never been to a literary
tea or cocktail party, and went in and out of New
York without seeing a reporter.[1] 'This excellent
quarantine I broke at the time of the Spanish
Civil War when I felt it was necessary to state
which side I believed to be right. There has never
been any quarantine since but it has been violated
very rarely and usually with disastrous results.'

I'll give Hemingway the final word. 'Some
critics are well-intentioned, most of them I believe. But some are not. When you ask understanding they bring envy and jealousy. Sometimes
they give off an odour that you only smell in the
armpits of the shirts of traitors after they have
been hanged. But these are the rare ones. I believe

---

[1] When William Faulkner came to New York on his way
to receive his Nobel Prize, he was met at the airport by a
female reporter who asked him what was the most decadent thing in modern life (this was smart city stuff to
catch the country boy, W. F. being dubbed 'a decadent')
He replied, 'What you're doing, miss.'

there is a segment of criticism which would be happier if there were no books written and if they could only write about each other and their own opinions. But perhaps nature, or God, will provide a bloody flux for which there will be no antidote and to which they only will be susceptible and it will do away with them.'

CHAPTER VI

WAR

THE popular idea of a Hemingway short story is given by Stephen Spender in an article in *Penguin New Writing*. 'War is good and real, violence is necessary, the only way of judging men is to find out whether they are tough or yellow.'[1] Let us go slowly and begin by admitting that Hemingway is at least fascinated by war. He has taken part in or observed five wars, all of his own choosing. He could have avoided war at close quarters had he wished—not an easy thing to do in this century.

We can look at the salient points of his war experience briefly. In the first World War he was rejected by the U.S. Army because of his injured eye but in the spring of 1918 he joined an ambulance unit destined for the Italian front. At Fossalte di Piave he was blown up by an Austrian trench-mortar bomb and had 237 pieces of iron in his leg. (They were still working their way out, thirty years later.) Carrying a legless Italian back to the trenches he was machine-gunned in the knee and ankle. He was awarded the Croce di Guerra with three citations and the Medaglio d'Argento al Valor Militare, second highest Italian military decoration, carrying with it a small pension. He returned to Oak Park in 1919 with an aluminium knee-cap.

He reported the Greco-Turkish War for the Toronto *Star*. He believes that he really learned

[1] 'Books and the War', *P.N.W.* No. 5.

about war in Asia Minor. It was there he saw the broken-legged baggage animals pitched into the harbour.

In Spain he was a correspondent. In the second World War he gained experience on land and sea and in the air. His 40-foot cabin cruiser, the *Pilar*, was transformed into a Q-boat and worked for Naval Intelligence. 1942-4 it cruised off the north coast of Cuba, locating submarines. Hemingway had a secret plan for destroying submarines, once hailed alongside, which he never was. He was recommended for a decoration in connection with this work. In 1944 he was accredited correspondent to the R.A.F. and flew with them on a number of operational missions.

His land service was officially as correspondent for *Collier's Weekly* accredited to the Third Army. He didn't like observing, so he only wrote enough articles to prevent being recalled, and he didn't like General Patton so he joined an American pursuit squadron in Normandy and then attached himself to the Fourth Infantry Division of the First Army. He kept ahead of it in his jeep and contacted the French irregulars. He appeared to be fighting his own war and once sent back word that if he was to hold out he would need tanks. He set up his headquarters in Rambouillet, dispensed justice, sent cycling patrols into the German lines, collected information. Moving on, his personal Task Force was skirmishing at the Arc de Triomphe when General Leclerc was still on the south bank. Later there was a controversy as to whether he should be decorated or court-martialled for contravention of the Geneva Convention governing the conduct of war correspondents. He was interrogated and acquitted and later received the Bronze Star.[1]

It is too easy to say a man likes war, although it is obvious that many do. It is not battle that men enjoy but the war situation, nineteen-twentieths of which is freedom from responsibility and relaxation of social discipline, or replacement by military discipline. But these things mean nothing to Hemingway. In the last war he sought responsibility. Moreover, there are always loopholes for a person of his reputation and status if he wishes to avoid responsibility, without endangering life and limb. The attraction of war is subtle. In few of Hemingway's war pictures is there any emotion. When it breaks through, as in 'On The Quai At Smyrna', it is distorted into irony. His aim seems to be the examination of men in a particular situation, perhaps a distasteful one, but nevertheless a common one. He is fascinated by men's fascination and for the study of this fascination he brings an attitude of acceptance. There are people who cry against war and spend their lives discovering a way to reject it, and theirs is an honourable way, but it is not his. His rôle is to observe but, because observation is useless without understanding, also to participate. In writing of war it is necessary to describe the horrors, the desolation, the heart-breakingness. But to maintain his rôle he must do it in a flat, deadpan way. 'At the start of the winter came the

[1] I am chiefly indebted to Malcolm Cowley's 'A Portrait of Mr. Papa', for this account of Hemingway's war experience.

permanent rain and with the rain came the cholera.
But it was checked and in the end only seven
thousand died of it in the army.'[1] To understand the
reality of war it is necessary to read Hemingway and
Sassoon almost simultaneously.

But why should people who presumably dislike
war adopt this attitude of acceptance? Hemingway
does it because he is a writer and to him war is a
landscape or a milieu. But why should others, who
can put the experience to no good use, also accept?
Acceptance is far more widespread than the solitary
attitude of a writer. Half the human race are shrug-
ging their shoulders. The machinery of war is so
immense the individuals that set it in motion are
dwarfed and become sharply conscious of their little-
ness. And then, of course, there is ordinary human
stupidity and the lack of spirit that causes men to
obey orders for the sake of immediate, individual
peace. Lieutenant Henry's drivers felt that they had
to accept the war, not from their stupidity but from
the inertia that overcomes the active intellect in wartime. Passini said there was nothing worse than war.
He was in favour of giving up, letting the enemy overrun the country and do their worst until they were
tired and went home. But it is significant that even
Passini stayed with his ambulance. Then the uncon-
querable stupidity.

> 'There is a class that controls a country that is
> stupid and does not realise anything and never can.
> That is why we have this war'.
> 'Also they make money out of it'.

[1] *Farewell To Arms.*

'Most of them don't', said Passini. 'They are too stupid. They do it for nothing. For stupidity'.[1]

Hemingway's natural objectivity must have been strengthened by the acceptance he found among the Italian soldiers. To describe a person he has always believed it necessary to become that person for a period, to see with his eyes and act upon his thoughts.

In a vague way Lieutenant Henry's driver was trying to apportion blame. They felt that war was wrong and unnecessary and behind it lay some colossal stupidity. The priest with whom Henry was on terms of uneasy friendship felt much the same as they, perhaps digging a little deeper, yet still baffled about causes and remedies. He put his views awkwardly in the conversation with Henry in hospital to which I have already referred. He senses a difference of attitude between the officers and men, something that existed prior to the war and caused one set to take commissions and the other set to stay in the ranks. 'What is the difference?' Henry asks.

> 'I cannot say it easily. There are people who would make war. In this country there are many like that. There are other people who would not make war'.
> 'But the first ones make them do it'.
> 'Yes'.
> 'And I help them'.
> 'You are a foreigner. You are a patriot!'
> 'And the ones who would not make war? Can they stop it?'
> 'I do not know'.
> He looked out of the window again. I watched his face.

[1] *Farewell To Arms.*

'Have they ever been able to stop it?'
'They are not organised to stop things and when they get organised their leaders sell them out'.
'Then it's hopeless?'
'It is never hopeless'.[1]

But it is not in the causes of war that you come across the enormous uncertainty. Historians and politicians have analysed them with great finality and yet, with the first breath of war, the finality dissolves and once again you are faced with the unanswerable question: Why are two highly armed sets of men moving against each other? And when they move, what happens? Another question which has rarely been answered. Few people have ever been able to tell us or even known what happens in battle. Moments are saturated with activity – mind, heart and muscle – and the reporter who can record them fully has not been born. The Generals know least of all. Their accounts are either stylised representations of what might have happened (as the traditional accounts of Quatre Bras and Waterloo) or verbal flounderings like the official Russian account of the Battle of Orel in the last war. The Colonel in *Across the River* tries to give Renata some sense of war, and apologises. 'You forgive me, Daughter. Much of what I say is unjust. But it is truer than the things you will read in Generals' memoirs. After a man gets one star, or more, the truth becomes as difficult for him to attain as the Holy Grail was in our ancestors' time.' It is the captains, he says, who know the exact truth and can often tell it.

[1] *Farewell To Arms.*

Hemingway has not a prejudice against Generals as such. He recognises that there must be Generals in an army just as Sassoon recognised there must be Base Officers. Some he admired, others he didn't. He has been widely credited with saying that 'generals are good people'. He showed his admiration for some of them long before the recent war.

> ... They buried a general who was shot through the head by a sniper. This is where those writers are mistaken who write books called *Generals Die in Bed*, because this general died in a trench dug in snow, high in the mountains, wearing an Alpini hat with an eagle feather in it and a hole in front you couldn't put your little finger in and a hole in back you could put your fist in, if it were a small fist and you wanted to put it there, and much blood in the snow. He was a damned fine general, and so was General von Behr who commanded the Bavarian Alpenkorps troops at the battle of Caporetto and was killed in his staff car by the Italian rearguard as he drove into Udine ahead of his troops, and the titles of all such books should be *Generals Usually Die in Bed*, if we are to have any sort of accuracy in such things.[1]

It is unusual for a writer to laud a general, even a good one. With his necessary love of free expression, a writer tends to make a general a symbol of those things that are hostile to a healthy literature – authority and its complement, implicit obedience. Perhaps Hemingway's self-imposed acceptance of war infected his judgment of other things, and just as he accepted war for literary purposes so he accepted the figure of the military leader. But it is more probable

[1] 'A Natural History of the Dead'.

that a greater enemy to literature is already on the scene and that, as has happened before, Hemingway was the first to see it. He has reserved his capacity for caricature for the delineation of Frederick Harrison, administrator and bureaucrat. Just as writers of the past gave unreal portraits of generals out of their hatred, so Hemingway gives us the impossible character of Harrison, talking his thoughts aloud as people never do.

Back in the first war one of the characters in *Farewell to Arms* had been impressed by the extent of knowledge a general must have. He had been jokingly told that he could be a general in the American Army and he replied, 'No, I don't know enough to be a general. A general's got to know a hell of a lot. You guys think there ain't anything to war. You ain't got brains enough to be a second-class corporal.'

This isn't Hemingway speaking but I think he's behind it. It helps us understand his fascination with war and his partiality for generals. I would even hazard a guess that, if he could live his life over again with the knowledge he already has, he might set out to be a general. More and more generals are reverting to the ancient rôle of governors and administrators. (Hemingway probably thinks that a soldier is better trained for administration than a civil servant.) Sophocles was made a general on the strength of his play. MacArthur was not made Poet Laureate on the strength of his generalship, but he was made an Emperor. With his all-embracing interest in humanity Hemingway wishes to participate in leadership as well as discipleship. With his great versatility he is fitted to take charge of big projects. There is a slight trace (he would not allow more to come to the surface) of wistfulness in some of his war writing. He has definite opinions on the ability of Allied generals in the recent war and he seems to be under some compulsion to publicise them (through his Colonel's mouth for instance). Eisenhower was 'strictly the Epworth League... An excellent politician. Political General. Very able at it.' Many never fought. Bradley and Lightning Joe were good. Montgomery and Patton were not.[1]

This discussion on generals may seem only a minor part of a discussion on war. But Hemingway does not treat the issues of war in the way made familiar by other writers. Accepting the existence of war he is chiefly concerned with the physical impact on the individual soldier and then those decisions which, far, far away, cause the impact. When he departs from this physical and tactical examination and puts war to the test of conscience, it is precisely at the time when his concept of political man is emerging. The first time we hear of a just war, implying other unjust wars, is in Spain. Robert Jordan starts to feel worried by the number of men he has killed – strange men, many of them from Navarra, the people he likes best in the whole of Spain. Without a conscience you kill people merely because you are told to. With a conscience you still kill them because you have been told to, but first of all you have to make a decision, to support one side rather than another for definite reasons, outside of war. Jordan

[1] *Across The River.*

was not in the Spanish War for motives of excitement
or adventure. It is still wrong to kill but you do it
because your cause is right. 'It is right, he told himself, not reassuringly but proudly. I believe in the
people and their right to govern themselves as they
wish. But you mustn't believe in killing, he told himself. You must do it as a necessity but you must not
believe in it. If you believe in it the whole thing is
wrong.'[1] And although his political faith could not
fit into any of the contemporary straitjackets, he
continued to believe that the enlargement of the
Spanish War still had a right and wrong to it. 'Most
of this last war made sense,' he said, 'while the first
one made little sense to me.'[2]

But so far we have been skirting the real problem of Hemingway's approach to war. It is easy to
sense the fascination but not nearly so easy to understand the core of that fascination. Acknowledging the
acceptance of war and the formation of a political
attitude that will contain war does not bring us any
nearer to the reality we seek. To find that reality it
is best to seek for something that exists in both his
war stories and in his stories of civilian life. That
thing is surely death, the end of life, how men approach it and what it means to them. One phrase I
have already recorded is significant: 'death and its
occasional temporary avoidance which we describe
as life'. Death not only on the battlefield but also in
the afternoon and in the bedroom and in the Gulf
of Mexico, death providing the background for life

[1] *For Whom the Bell Tolls.*
[2] Quoted by Malcolm Cowley, 'A Portrait of Mr. Papa'.

and not vice versa. In the back of his mind, perhaps, the feeling that we are dead much longer than we are alive. John Peale Bishop wrote that Hawthorne had dramatised the human soul and Hemingway its disappearance. The disappearance of the soul is not to be envisaged simply as modern paganism, the passing away into an utter void, but as a state where the soul is starved during life, withering away through lack of sustenance. To get the full flavour of this we must link the desolation of the battlefield with the desolation of post-war life, with its absence of value and aim and hope. I don't know how true this is but Bishop puts it very well.

> The most tragic thing about the war was not that it made so many dead men, but that it destroyed the tragedy of death. Not only did the young suffer in the war, but every abstraction that would have sustained and given dignity to their suffering. The war made the traditional morality inacceptible; it did not annihilate it; it revealed its immediate inadequacy. So that at its end, the survivors were left to face, as they could, a world without values.[1]

I think I have made it clear that I do not agree completely with this interpretation of the Lost Generation. It is, I feel, too subtle. That the most tragic thing about modern war is that is has destroyed the tragedy of death I believe to be true, but for reasons different from Bishop's. Tragedy should be and always has been an individual matter. It only exists when one is aware of the personality destroyed. But there is no personality in modern war. It is, for the most part, literally anonymous. Robert Jordan was

[1] *The Collected Essays of John Peale Bishop.*

aware of it. It made it more difficult for him to acquiesce. Edwin Muir noted the mechanical quality in 'The Killers'. Here the potential killing was not to be anonymous but it was to be carried out in as impersonal a manner as possible. It is this quality, I feel, that lies at the root of Hemingway's feeling about war. In the face of such vast numbers, veiling their identity, he can only remark laconically that a mere seven thousand died of cholera and that it was a nice business when the broken-legged mules were pushed into the harbour.

But I believe that altogether too much fuss has been made over the Lost Generation. Hemingway is always represented as tolling their knell to the accompaniment of *Götterdämmerung* drinking. Emphasis is always laid on lack of this, that and the other. History has proved the thesis wrong. The Lost Generation (or one-hundred-thousandth part of it) was having a well-earned party. After a spell of active service men are apt to get drunk, and their action is viewed with tolerance. After a disaster such as a major war, lasting four years, men and women are apt to get drunk for a commensurate period. There is always a Fitzgerald whose constitution will not be equal to the test. But what about the emergence of Hemingway as a serious writer of the first class? Of Ford producing his Tietjens trilogy, Dos Passos his U.S.A. novels, Cummings his poetry? Buckingham and Rochester were more hopelessly lost than any of these ever were.

Hemingway is interested in war for what it does to men at the time rather than for what it may do to them afterwards. He saw what fear could do to them – and I shall devote the next chapter to this important subject. It could deprive them of their wits, reduce them to animals – or 'natural men', in Muir's phrase. During the panic that was Caporetto, Lieutenant Henry saw officers being arrested indiscriminately and shot, simply as a recoil from a dangerous situation. 'I saw how their minds worked; if they had minds and if they worked. They were all young men and they were saving their country.'[1] It is doubtful if even this rationalisation existed; action was the only response they were capable of, thought was beyond them.

And yet there could be good in it. Good even in the evil he noticed in another context. For instance, the anonymity. Applying that to yourself, to the individual soldier, he lost his identity and became a cipher. For the normal purposes of living this is a horror, one of the major successes of barbarism in a machine-ridden society. But in war, when you stand naked, one of a host standing for what you believe against what you are convinced is evil, it can be a boon. You are no longer yourself, you are part of a cause, or a crusade. You rid yourself of self, you become an instrument in the employment of good, as self-sacrificing as the true elect of Christian days. And strangely enough, you cease to hate. You become so engrossed in your own ordained rôle you forget the enemy, perhaps even the aim, but that is because you have satisfied yourself on that long ago and no longer need to think of it. 'Once you saw it

[1] *Farewell To Arms.*

again as it was to others, once you got rid of your own self, the always ridding of self that you had to do in war. When there could be no self. Where yourself is only to be lost.'[1]

Also, on a different, more homely level but perhaps just as important, war did something to bring the best uppermost in man. Hemingway compares the soldier with the politician, to the latter's disadvantage. They belong to the same species and they are in the same thing together; only their rôles differ. The politician lives by words and wallows in garrulity. He would shape the world by words—not carefully chosen, significant words, as writers should use and sometimes do, but always clichés and usually self-deceiving lies, borrowed from Demosthenes and Burke and Gladstone. The soldier is brought face to face with the bare bones of existence sometimes literally the skeleton, and he knows that the important words denote the things he knows, not the things he has dreamed. There is nothing wrong with the dreamer providing he is not garrulous. The politician captured in *The Fifth Column* hopes to save himself with a flood of words; they have rescued him frequently from tight corners before. But the man they left by the wayside 'was a soldier and he would never have talked. I would have liked the questioning of him, but such a business is useless'. Probably a piece of romanticism but the contrast remains true.

War moves through phases of unreality. The most familiar is the reported war, in which soldiers are sometimes unbearably loquacious the plays and

[1] *For Whom The Bell Tolls.*

novels of the past where they stated their war aims in faultless periods. The Greek drama indulged in it but as there was no attempt at realism – not even the idea existed – it is an acceptable framework. But when later writers attempted to combine realism with military romanticism we were given a distasteful hybrid of mangled bodies uttering magnificent sentiments. None of Hemingway's soldiers utter these sentiments; the nearest they get to it is a somewhat self-conscious internal monologue about why they consider it their business to fight, after Robert Jordan. Frederick Henry did not even go as far as that:

> I was always embarrassed by the words sacred, glorious and sacrifice and the expression in vain. We had heard them, sometimes standing in the rain almost out of earshot, so that only the shouted words came through, and had read them, on proclamations that were slapped up by billposters over other proclamations, now for a long time, and I had seen nothing sacred, and the things that were glorious had no glory and the sacrifices were like the stockyards at Chicago if nothing was done with the meat except to bury it.[1]

The glory words are not usually used by soldiers though some adopt them because they think it is part of the routine of war like saluting to the left and other bits of military nonsense. Each generation invents its new stock of glory words and for a time many people cannot see their falsity. A good example is the vocabulary expended on guerilla and partisan units during the last war. Few journalists (except the Russians) were crude enough to employ the old faded

[1] *Farewell To Arms.*

speech counters but new ones were brought into use and rapidly became just as drained of vitality as the old ones. The new method was to demonstrate the partisan's determination, courage and political rightness not by verbal inflation but by an incoherent species of understatement, a form of expression that comes easily to the Anglo-Saxon journalist. There is a dualism in Hemingway's attitude to the Spanish partisans which is weighted rather on the side of the new glamorisation but is modified by a more critical approach. Under his close scrutiny the partisans are seen to be fighting for a number of reasons, not all of them politically respectable. Some enjoy the life, others fight from inertia – they happened to be in a particular place at a particular time. Robert Jordan saw this; when it was necessary for Pablo's group to fight it was not because they sought action but because the action had been brought to 'this lazy outfit'. It is the writer who has the harder job. He has to put it all down on paper and satisfy many men, all of them himself at different times. A man cannot be true to truth all the time.

Then there were moments when, although officially and technically involved, you could stand aside and be a spectator. The feeling would come over Lieutenant Henry that he would not be killed. Not in this war. It did not have anything to do with me. It seemed no more dangerous to me myself than war in the movies.'[1] He was fighting on 'the picturesque front'. When he stood away from things and tried to get a picture of the whole front the result was even

[1] *Farewell To Arms.*

laughable. 'The Italians had crossed and spread out a little way on the far side to hold about a mile and a half on the Austrian side of the river. It was a nasty place and the Austrians should not have let them hold it. I suppose it was mutual tolerance because the Austrians still kept a bridgehead further down the river.'[1] So there were many aspects of war none of them glorious but some of them amusing or picturesque or cinematic, depending on where you were and how you felt. There was naturally the games analogy. 'War had been to him like football. American football. What they play at the colleges' (*The Torrents of Spring*).

In addition to undraping the human body and tongue war also tore off the conventions of habit and custom. The proprieties were dropped. When a comrade thanked Philip politely, Philip replied (with a certain amount of pomposity it must be admitted), 'Oh don't say thank you in a war. This is a war. You don't say thank you in it.'[2] This is Hemingway trundling his cart a little too hard. It is an attitude as distasteful as the glory one and reminds me of a Major who used to storm into our billets at six o'clock in the morning in midwinter shouting, 'Come on, up you get! Yes I know! War is hell!' – but he had a sense of irony. In fact, as a more democratic attitude is painfully being introduced into our armies there is a slight increase in politeness—officers sometimes say Please. My point here is that, although war strips a man of his shams, Hemingway occasionally tends to flay him for full measure.

[1] *Ibid.* [2] *The Fifth Column.*

I said earlier that there is no need to assume that
Hemingway likes war. The attitude is one of fascination, not necessarily of liking. According to Sam Boal,
Hemingway does not like war. He calls it 'the sad
science, *le métier triste*', and puts these words into the
mouth of the Colonel in *Across the River*. The truth
can only be discovered when we realise that war is
not a unity but is composed of many things. For my
own part I like the companionship but detest the
discipline. I find it difficult to believe that Hemingway
found anything but pleasure in his patrolling of the
Western Theatre or his sailing off Cuba, but one can
get these enjoyments without setting the world to
slaughter. But war is part of our lives and no serious
writer can ignore it. It was right for Trollope to ignore
it for it scarcely existed in his day but now there is
a difference. Hemingway writes of war and 'he talks
tirelessly about war – all War – not just his wars,
which he realises are boring to most other people'.[1]

The germ of his fascination must surely have
been planted on the Italian front when

> We took this young man with his sensitive genius for
> experience, for living all the qualities of life and find-
> ing a balance among them – and with that too obvious
> fear in him of proving inadequate – and we shoved him
> into our pit of slaughter, and told him to be courageous
> about killing. And we thought he would come out
> weeping and jittering. Well, he came out roaring for
> blood, shouting to the skies the joy of killing, the
> 'religious ecstasy' of killing – and most pathetic, most
> pitiable, killing as a protest against death.[2]

[1] Sam Boal, 'I Tell You True', *Park East*.
[2] Max Eastman, *Art and the Life of Action*.

His closeness to death remained a horror which never left him until he discovered that death can only be overcome by inoculation–death is defeated by the administration of death. To give death is a godlike attribute. The man who gives it does not kneel to death but gains the right of mastership over it. Hemingway reinforces this mystical interpretation by reference to the undoubted delight that has been felt by many human beings in the bequest of death. He admits that he himself enjoys killing. This is the education, as he calls it, that has been given to the young men of Europe, Asia and America over the last two generations. The eclipse of standards, about which so much fuss has been made, was in many cases temporary. The obsession with death is becoming permanent.

Whatever the experience, Hemingway tries to extract value from it for his writing. War is of course no exception and in one of his two books of literary criticism he acknowledges the debt he feels to war. Of Tolstoy's *Sevastopol* he writes:

> It was a very young book and had one fine description in it, where the French take the redoubt and I thought about Tolstoy and what a great advantage an experience of war was to a writer. It was one of the major subjects and certainly one of the hardest to write truly of and those writers who had not seen it were always very jealous and tried to make it seem unimportant, or abnormal, or a disease as a subject, while, really, it was just something quite irreplaceable that they had missed.[1]

[1] *Green Hills of Africa.*

CHAPTER VII

THE MECHANICS OF FEAR

THE numbing sensation of fear is a central feature of Hemingway's work. Its expression rises quite naturally out of his war experience, but something congenital and deeper in his personality gives it especial significance. Many critics have approached this when referring to his competitiveness and his need to prove himself but I have never seen a full examination of the emotion-in-action.

First let us rid ourselves of the superficial view that the generation for which Hemingway spoke during the early part of his career was exceptionally subject to fear. This has been suggested by J. Donald Adams when he wrote, with that brand of self-satisfaction that professional reviewers assume as an outer skin, that 'we have already had our literary generation which surrendered to fears; it called itself the Lost Generation. Let us not have another.'[1]

Whether Mr. Adams likes it or not, we have had and will have others. Probably the best answer to him is contained in Wellington's statement that the man who says he is not afraid in battle is a damned liar, or some such phrase. The generation that fought in the 1914-18 war (a much more horrifying experience than the last one) was badly scared. Perhaps a few escaped, but we are discussing normal, sensitive men. For some years the generation was branded and nothing they could do could hide it. But they grew

[1] *Literary Frontiers.*

out of the fear just as they managed to reorient themselves in other spheres of adaptation.

Everyone who knows Hemingway agrees that his wound in Italy marked him for life, spiritually as well as physically. The shock of this wound was so great that he has spent a large part of the rest of his life trying to assure himself that he is not scared. So far from luxuriating in his wound, as people like Adams imply, he has steeled himself to recover his normality. The discipline of his writing is perhaps a reflection of this other discipline in his mental life. When he was wounded he told a friend, 'I felt my soul or something coming right out of my body, like you'd pull a silk handkerchief out of a pocket by one corner. It flew around and then came back and went in again and I wasn't dead any more.' For a long time after that he was afraid to sleep in the dark. 'In the early years,' writes Malcolm Cowley, 'he forced himself to walk forward into danger because of his competitive spirit and because he was proving to himself that he was not that scared.'[1] (When camping, T. E. Lawrence used to sleep out in the rain just to satisfy himself that he could do it.)

Whenever Hemingway is writing of failure he usually ascribes it to fear. However it may be veiled it is the basic cause. A woman breaks from the embrace of an amorous matador and says, 'These are the hungry people. A failed bullfighter. With your ton-load of fear. If you have so much of that, use it in the ring.'[2] In the same story the dishwasher Enrique knows that he could never be a bullfighter

[1] 'Portrait of Mr. Papa'.   [2] 'The Capital of the World'.

because of his fear. He sculptures four perfect veronicas with his apron and finishes up with a rebolera.

> 'Look at that', he said. 'And I wash dishes'.
> 'Why?'
> 'Fear', said Enrique. 'Miedo. The same fear you would have in a ring with a bull'.

The bullfighters know only too well that fear is their greatest enemy. Not the bull, but their own fear of the bull. Once fear creeps upon them they lose whatever is special to them. 'Bullfighters say that fear of a bull takes the type away from a bullfighter, that is, if he is arrogant and bossy, or easy and graceful, fear removes these characteristics.'[1] Once a man loses the thing that sets him apart, the thing that forms personality and creates individuality, he is lost. He sinks back into the herd and he will never excel in anything he puts his hand or mind to. Fear cannot be hidden, no matter how it decks itself; the bullfighter who was repulsed by the woman eventually lost her to a picador. His fear stood out and made him repulsive.

For some years Hemingway suffered this agony. He created Jake Barnes, his counterpart whose self-lack was entirely physical. But however hopeless Jake's predicament, it was certain. There was no turning back and there was no recovery. He knew exactly where he was and he could at least make the effort of adjustment. Hemingway's situation was different. Jake had nothing left to fear – he *was* impotent, he had no doubts on that score. Hemingway

[1] *Death in the Afternoon.*

believed he had been face to face with death, in the vivid classical metaphor. He didn't know whether he dared face death again. Nor is it an easy matter to put it to the test. A man who fears sexual impotence can settle the question quite simply. A man who fears his own fear can put himself in danger but he can never be sure how he acquits himself. A certain degree of fear is normal and wholesome. How can a man know what this degree might be? Hemingway sought violence and brutality in an attempt to dissolve his doubts. While his legs healed he examined his mind anxiously. He found the bullring. This was a vicarious experience yet it was something not to turn away in horror or be sickened like so many Anglo-Saxons. It was a manner of dealing death, defying death and with it the fear of death.

But watching bullfights could not provide a complete exorcism. Not even by becoming one of the leading aficionados in Spain could he purge himself wholly. And so when he returned to Spain in 1937 he was still sick; 'he came with the apprehension of a man who has been hurt and twisted by the Great War and who was now voluntarily exposing himself to bombs and shells, afraid of being afraid once more and eager to share the experience of a people's struggle.'[1]

The Macomber story, probably his best known, has fear for its characteristic situation. Macomber has shown fear – he has run away from a lion. The story concerns his attempt to rehabilitate himself in the eyes of his wife and the white hunter. From that

[1] Arturo Barea, 'Not Spain But Hemingway'.

moment onwards he must not only cease to betray his fear but he must also show positive courage. V.C.s have told us that in the moment of courage they were actually in a state of panic, and this is generally accepted. But no such comforting rationalisation of the reality of courage can satisfy the individual who has been discovered in the act of cowardice. Hemingway's problem was a peculiar one. He had not been discovered in any act of cowardice but he himself knew that he had been frightened. One part of him accused the other and insisted on reparation.

There is an insistence throughout this story that fear is not to be condoned. Among the Christian virtues is courage but fear is not rated as a sin. Indeed, the Christian is expected to show fear in certain situations, else he will be accused of pride. But Hemingway, Macomber and especially Mrs. Macomber are driven by a hard logic to regard fear as a sin that must be punished mercilessly. Macomber's fear was, of course, extreme and was expressed in an act of cowardice – yet cowardice is not a scientific term and in their hearts many people would sympathise with Macomber and regard his cowardice as justified. Not so his wife. After Wilson had killed the lion she

> had not looked at him nor he at her and he had sat by her in the back seat with Wilson sitting on the front seat. Once he had reached over and taken his wife's hand without looking at her and she had removed her hand from his. Looking across the steam to where the gunbearers were skinning out the lion he could see that she had been able to see the whole thing. While they sat there his wife had reached forward and put

her hand on Wilson's shoulder. He turned and she
had leaned forward over the low seat and kissed him
on the mouth.

Macomber's fear deserved the bitterest humiliation.
The coward is a familiar character in Hemingway's work but he is never the traditional cringing
coward. He is often a person who some of us would
not call a coward at all. But the word or at least the
thought springs readily to lips or mind. The dying
man in 'The Snows of Kilimanjaro' is called a coward
by his wife because he doesn't want to move. She is
accusing him of accepting the end too tranquilly, she
wants him to struggle. In *For Whom the Bell Tolls*
we get a careful study of a confessed coward, Pablo.
He is interesting because he admits his cowardice;
it is quite clear how he has arrived at his condition,
clear to himself and to us. But the epithet is not
easily borne. The contempt for cowardice is so strong
in our tradition we struggle against it even when we
know it is a reality. When Pilar calls Pablo a coward
he is offended.

> 'Coward', Pablo said bitterly. 'You treat a man as
> coward because he has a tactical sense. Because he
> can see the results of an idiocy in advance. It is not
> cowardly to know what is foolish'.
> 'Neither is it foolish to know what is cowardly', said
> Anselmo, unable to resist making the phrase.

Fear and its result in action, cowardice, being
so common, attempts are always being made to interpret them as something else. Pablo denies the charge
and had he been English might have said, 'Discretion

is the better part of valour'. Or it can be dramatised, the shame buried in laughter, as in *The Good Soldier Schweik*. Today, when the language of heroism has become deflated, it is even fashionable to assert one's own cowardice, but there is an implicit agreement that this is a pose. We still have not reached the stage where fear, a spiritual wound, is viewed as tolerantly as a physical wound. Even the members of Pablo's partisan group, who realised that their leader's condition was something over which he had no more control than over a running nose, could not pardon him. They stated his malady accurately yet scornfully. 'In the first days of the movement and before too, he was something. Something serious. But now he is finished. The plug has been drawn and the wine has all run out of the skin.' A flesh wound heals, a broken limb mends. But fear feeds on itself and there is no surety of recovery. It follows a law resembling geometric progression. Once the original fear is planted a second fear branches, a fear that the first fear has become permanent. Then comes a third fear, that one's whole psyche has been poisoned.

One of the clearest accounts of how fear can disable a personality is to be found in this book. The partisans are discussing divination. For Robert Jordan the evil prognostications are always the product of fear.

> 'I believe that fear produces evil visions', Robert Jordan said. 'Seeing bad signs –'.
> 'Such as the airplanes today', Primitivo said.
> 'Such as thy arrival', Pablo said softly and Robert Jordan looked across the table at him, saw it was not a

provocation but only an expressed thought, then went on. 'Seeing bad signs, one, with fear, imagines an end for himself and one thinks that imagining comes by divination', Robert Jordan concluded. 'I believe there is nothing more to it than that. I do not believe in ogres, nor soothsayers, nor in supernatural things'.

'But this one with the rare name saw his fate clearly', the gypsy said. 'And that was how it happened'.

'He did not see it', Robert Jordan said. 'He had a fear of such a possibility and it became an obsession. No one can tell me that he saw anything'.

It is probably safe to assume that everyone has his fears but they are restricted to particular fields and are therefore intermittent in their action. (The films are fond of this; many an actor has enjoyed portraying the sudden transformation of a fearless man into a knock-kneed coward at the sight of a lipstick-stained coffee cup or a nurse's apron.) The pit of fear is descended when a man's whole personality is warped, when he is nothing but fear on legs. Hemingway's best instance is Eddy, the rummy in *To Have and Have Not*, who can only approach normality by having his fear soaked out of him. 'I gave him a real one. I knew they wouldn't make him drunk now; not pouring them into all that fear.' (It is interesting to hear that a number of rummies figure among his close circle of friends; with a character like Hemingway in the vicinity it is probably worthwhile becoming a professional rummy. He will study them as closely as a psychoanalyst studies his pet Oedipus complex.) But drink is only effective for a very short time. 'It certainly was wonderful what a drink would do to him and how quick.' It didn't last long though.

The chief consolation is that fear can be overcome. All the multiplying fears can be destroyed by going to the root of the original one. Macomber discovered this when, after the lion episode, he steeled himself to face wild beasts again without shrinking. The fear fled from him as quickly as though it had been attacked by alcohol, but there was no need for it to return. It was not merely hiding. He could not conceal his elation at the defeat of his great enemy.

> Macomber's face was shining. 'You know, something did happen to me', he said. 'I feel absolutely different'.

To Wilson it was just as if Macomber was coming of age. He saw a fear that had perhaps only been brought out by the lion but probably much, much older now, being put to flight.

> Beggar had probably been afraid all his life. Don't know what started it. But over now. Hadn't had time to be afraid with the buff. That and being angry too. Motor car too. Motor cars make it familiar. Be a damn fire eater now. He'd seen it in the war work the same way. More of a change than any loss of virginity. Fear gone like an operation. Something else grew in its place. Main thing a man had. Made him into a man. Women knew it too. No bloody fear.

As for the genesis of fear, after which Wilson groped, only complete knowledge can reveal it. Even when we think we have traced it to a particular event, to an explosion in war or the face of a lion or some insignificant occurrence in the nursery, we may still be cheating ourselves. The event may be no more than the occasion on which a primal fear became

objective. Fear may be in the human heritage. Like
the waiter in 'A Clean, Well-Lighted Place', we may
be afraid of the void. Fear of the dark may be a
memory of nothing. Fear of solitude may be fear of
the thing we came from and, at least symbolically,
return to. 'What did he fear? It was not fear or dread.
It was a nothing that he knew too well. It was all
a nothing and a man was nothing too. It was only
that and light was all it needed and a certain clean-
ness and order. Some lived it and never felt it but he
knew it was all nada y pues nada y nada y pues nada.'[1]
How is this fear to be purged? If you are convinced
that your whole existence is nada there is nothing
you can do about it. It is like war.

Or the whole thing may be based on a vast,
cosmic misunderstanding. We may be like the little
boy patiently waiting to die because his temperature
has soared impossibly far beyond forty-four degrees.

> 'About how long will it be before I die?'
> 'You aren't going to die. What's the matter with you?'
> 'Oh yes I am. I heard him say a hundred and two'.
> 'People don't die with a fever of one hundred and
> two. That's a silly way to talk'.
> 'I know they do. At school in France the boys told
> me you can't live with forty-four degrees. I've got a
> hundred and two'.
> He had been waiting to die all day, ever since nine
> o'clock in the morning.
> 'You poor Schatz', I said. 'Poor old Schatz. It's like
> miles and kilometres. You aren't going to die. That's a
> different thermometer. On that thermometer thirty-
> seven is normal. On this kind it's ninety-eight'.[2]

[1] From *Winner Take Nothing*.
[2] 'A Day's Wait', from *Winner Take Nothing*.

We may be fooling ourselves all the time. Those who fear nothingness may be psychotic cases. Those who fear death may be using the wrong thermometer. Those who fear their own fear may still be romantic primitives. But the folly is no greater than the folly of envying another person his new car or having nothing better to do than lean out of the window and at this moment the world is in turmoil for that very reason – and a few others.

CHAPTER VIII

THE LIFE OF DESPAIR

Answering one of my questions Hemingway wrote, 'We, as citizens, are governed by fear and guided by frustration, using a non-corrected compass.' He advised me to finish it myself, apparently on the grounds that any modern citizen will know what he is getting at.

His titles alone suggest frustration. *Men Without Women. Winner Take Nothing. To Have and Have Not.* Even *For Whom the Bell Tolls. The Sun Also Rises*, restored to its context in *Ecclesiastes*, breathes the same spirit. 'Vanity of vanities ... all is vanity. ... One generation passeth and another generation cometh; but the earth abideth forever. The sun also riseth, and the sun goeth down, and hasteth to the place where he arose.' God proposes, the temperament disposes. The Scottish poet, William Soutar, found hope in the notion that 'the earth abideth forever'. But for Hemingway God is a Gulf Stream, assimilating everything and uncaring. Hemingway is a very up-to-date Hardy. He writes as Hardy wanted to write (philosophically, of course) after the public had learnt to stomach *Jude The Obscure*. For Hemingway men never possess women in the way they would like to – either the woman is unready or, much more likely, circumstances are unfavourable. All winners suffer at the hands of the Great Illusion. In *Farewell, Bell* and *To Have and Have Not* the lovers are frustrated by death.

All plans are nullified by death. You know that
death is waiting so you know that hope is a mirage.
Even those people who win their hopes are frustrated
in the end for once you have got the thing you want
you wish to keep it and that is impossible. The
Eumenides have their eyes on you. Waiting for
Catherine to die Frederick Henry realised the bitter
truth, realised that until that moment his own life
had been mocking him.

> Now Catherine would die. That was what you did.
> You died. You did not know what it was about. You
> never had time to learn. They threw you in and told
> you the rules and the first time they caught you off
> base they killed you. Or they killed you gratuitously
> like Aymo. Or gave you the syphilis like Rinaldi. But
> they killed you in the end. You could count on that.
> Stay around and they would kill you.[1]

This is from the saddest episode in modern literature. No classical storming against the Fates. You
could not smother your despair, your bitterness, but
you had to take it lying down. Stay around and they
would kill you.

No one escapes. Even when he was very happy
with Catherine he seemed to have a premonition of
the end. Everyone dies but the happy die first. The
Lord thy God is a jealous God – thou must worship
no one but Him, not even Happiness, especially not
Happiness. Catherine must die because God envied
her courage.

> If people bring so much courage to this world the
> world has to kill them to break them, so of course it

[1] From *Farewell To Arms*.

147

kills them. The world breaks everyone and afterwards many are strong at the broken places. But those that will not break it kills. It kills the very good and the very gentle and the very brave impartially. If you are none of these you can be sure it will kill you too but there will be no special hurry.

And near the end Catherine realises this herself.

'I'm not brave any more, darling. I'm all broken. They've broken me. I know it now'.
'Everybody is that way'.
'But it's awful. They just keep it up till they break you'.

Hemingway is so explicit on the subject this chapter writes itself, or rather it has already been written. This suddenly brings me up against the embarrassing truth that a man writes his own work and what business have I to try and do it for him or explain things which he has explained better? God forgive me, I am trying to do homage to a great writer. *Farewell to Arms* is such a fine novel its mere contemplation rocks my emotion. I had better quote again. 'Catherine had a good time in the time of pregnancy. It wasn't bad. She was hardly ever sick. She was not awfully uncomfortable until toward the last. So now they got her in the end. You never get away with anything.' The message is drummed, drummed, drummed.

You are compelled to be cynical. Nothing will ever persuade you again that you can win. Even a rainbow will remind you of future storms. The young soldier learns this and the bullfighter knows it. The bullfighter knows that the end may come at any moment. No matter how skilled and famous he is, his end will come. Even if he avoids death in the ring he will grow old and clumsy and will die in bed. Once he has wiped out his adolescent dreams and ceased to be devout he will be a freer man. Dreams and devotion are a heavy burden to carry. To cease to worry, hope and scheme is to have time in which to live, or enjoy that part of life allotted him. Hemingway says the cynical ones are the best company. Just as one can only come to terms with a young man when his impossible idealism has been rooted out.

Nevertheless, it is very easy to apportion the blame wrongly. It is very easy to lay all blame at the door of the Fates or God, which really means the world, which really means other people – unless you believe in a Divine Plan. But belief in a Divine Plan that casts you for the rôle of hunted hare is a more terrible belief than that which holds your fellow men responsible. And in moments of honesty you realise that your fellow men are very much like you and whatever characteristics they have you are likely to have too. The attack is not altogether external. We play our own part. As members of the human race we do our bit in the progress to perdition. When Rinaldi fetched drinks for himself and Lieutenant Henry he poured out half a tumbler of cognac each.

> 'Too much', I said and held up the glass and sighted at the lamp on the table.
> 'Not for an empty stomach. It is a wonderful thing. It burns out the stomach completely. Nothing is worse for you'.

'All right'.

'Self destruction day by day', Rinaldi said. 'It ruins the stomach and makes the hand shake. Just the thing for a surgeon'.

'You recommend it?'

'Heartily. I use no other. Drink it down, baby, and look forward to being sick'.

In the days of faith it was termed diabolism. Now it seems as wise a course as any other – for how can there be wisdom?

Harry Morgan learnt a similar lesson, although in different terms. He also discovered that plans eventually fail, even when the early stages are successful. There was no idealistic background to Harry Morgan, he had the advantage of being a cynic from the beginning (as far as we can judge) and had no need to go through the usual process of disillusionment. Yet even he believed that certain things could be done and had to find that 'they would get him in the end'. Morgan's way was to pit himself against the rest. His last discovery was that one man is too weak to accomplish his designs. He appeared to be groping after some conception of organised effort, but by then he was already dying.

'A man', Harry Morgan said, looking at them both. 'One man alone ain't got. No man alone now'. He stopped. 'No matter how a man alone ain't got no bloody chance'.

He shut his eyes. It had taken him a long time to get it out and it had taken him all of his life to learn it.[1]

So far I have illustrated the emptiness of life as

[1] *To Have and Have Not.*

seen by Hemingway's character from the mind of a
soldier in the Great War and that of a Key West
though some twenty years later. In between lay the
Lost Generation who made this sense of emptiness
the basis of their lives. To borrow a word from one
of the stories, they lived in a world of nada, nothingness, Ancient Chaos re-enacted. What were once considered the most sacred subjects had lost meaning.
You could not take the Ten Commandments seriously when bishops exhorted you to kill and knew
that rape and plunder were inevitable concomitants.
You could no longer believe in political idealism
when none of the promises were honoured. You could
not honour love when it became hopelessly confused
with easy sex. The Lost Generation did not create
this hell, they were its victims. At first they wanted
to laugh but they soon grew tired of that. They ended
by finding it impossible either to revere or mock,
and just cut these things out of their lives. Jake's war-
wound was once funny. Brett had found it a joke.

> 'I laughed about it too, myself, once'. She wasn't
> looking at me. 'A friend of my brother's came home
> that way from Mons. It seemed like a hell of a joke.
> · Chaps never know anything, do they?'
> 'No', I said. 'Nobody ever knows anything'.

John W. Aldridge gives a very good summary
of what had happened to the Lost Generation in his
book *After the Lost Generation*. It would be pointless
to paraphrase so I give it in full.

> The war wrenched them away from the land of their
> childhood. It carried them forward in the long process

of disinheritance which began in school, when they were divested of their local customs and beliefs, and continued through their college years when they each took on the stamp of fragile aestheticism that eventually made them more at home in Gertrude Stein's salon than on Main Street. As spectators, guests of the war by courtesy of the management, they were infected with irresponsibility, thrilled at second hand by danger, held to a pitch of excitement that made their old lives seem impossibly dull and tiresome. As participants, they learned to view all life, all human emotion, in terms of war, to pursue pleasure with an intensity made greater by the constant threat of death, and to hold tight to themselves and to the concrete simplicities (until the simple and concrete seemed to be all there was, all that was worth knowing) when the world around them seemed to be breaking to pieces. If the war hurt them, as it hurt Frederick Henry, they became numb and stopped thinking and believing. It was not their war any more. If love died they stopped believing in love too and began believing in sex. If everything collapsed and they were left with nothing, that too was alright. They began believing in nothing.

The last sentence is the key one. Most commentators usually stop here, or they ask themselves how *they* would feel if they believed in nothing and come to the conclusion that it would be a horrifying state of mind. On the whole the Lost Generation did not, judging by their lives and speech, suffer the agonies they were supposed to. Undoubtedly the curtain is raised occasionally and we glimpse, for instance, Lady Brett miserable with the remorse of remembering the people she has hurt. It is extremely difficult to catch Bill Gorton and Mike Campbell out in this way. I feel that most of us are too easily

the slaves of traditional values. When we see them
broken we assume that the void that remains is a
terrifying one. But this conception of despair is
entirely *a priori*. It is true, these people do feel despair but it is a cold despair -- I almost said without
the passion that most people fling into their despair.
The term despair is heavy with emotional connota-
tions. The despair of the Lost Generation is little
more than a calm acquiescence in meaninglessness,
or a conviction that things are pretty bloody. Having
overthrown the gods they are not likely to shudder
at the gods' dictation.

Regarding Hemingway's work as a serial story
(which is possible, with the reservations I have men-
tioned earlier) Frederick Henry becomes Jake
Barnes and Catherine Barkley becomes Lady Brett.
Frederick and Catherine, despite the pose of life-
omniscience that they wear (it is worn by most people
who are in the thick of war, more for its protective
quality than for its dramatic attraction) are essentially fresh and even unspoilt personalities. When
they are together this reality is uppermost. With
Rinaldi, Frederick plays a different rôle because all
men must adjust themselves to their companions for
the sake of harmony. When the officers are baiting
the priest, Henry's true personality fights against its
mask. Jake Barnes has lived through this phase. He
has been hurt, the freshness has been knocked out of
him, and he has learnt to accept the prevailing law
of frustration. The question that arises is this: has
he adopted for good the mask of insentience that was
so useful in war, or has he actually become insentient?

The first alternative is usually assumed. I am not so sure. I think that Jake has had his emotions worn away, although there are occasional outcroppings such as occur in geological structures. And when you consider that this is a normal process, that the young man's love of poetry declines into indifference, that love itself sidles into affection, that political idealism is transformed into something we call realism – why should it be considered remarkable or shocking that Jake should be like other men? Jake is a genuine personality, more free of masks than most of us. Those who accuse him and his friends of surrender are usually those who have not dared to admit their own surrender.

The *Observer* Profile saw a Hemingway character as a man who faced the Fates grimly and (the paradox was not noticed by the author) undespairingly.

> It is a posture of despair held bolt upright by courage and virility. Despair is assumed *a priori*. The human situation, or at least the contemporary human situation is so obviously desperate that why it is so, how it became so, or (for Hemingway's Left-wing period never fitted into the myth) how to make it less so, are questions which never need to be discussed. If two Hemingway characters meet for the first time – as likely as not it will be in a bar – all this has been long ago assumed by both of them. Life is Godawful. Have another drink. It is really this facile and overwhelming assumption which makes the conversation of these people so dull.

Again, the understanding of the state we call despair is not quite true. It is a magpie. It is despair as seen by a man who does not despair or is trying desperately hard to pretend he does not despair. Despair was brought into the world by the Christians, it being the inevitable complement to their faith. As I shall illustrate later Hemingway in feeling is a pagan. More people than is implied by the author of the Profile hold views about life similar to a Hemingway character's, but believe it necessary to cling to a more respectable idiom. Part of our confusion today comes from our application of one set of terms and values to behaviour of quite a different species. The true despair is that of a churchman's when he urges men on to slaughter. The priest in *Farewell to Arms* is a most pathetic character. Hemingway's people have jettisoned the very faith that breeds despair. How can a non-Christian be plagued by Christian doubts? Jake Barnes and his friends have ceased to believe in all the old noble purposes. For this reason they are mentally at ease (though the ease may be stagnation) and enjoy life in the way they know is attainable. I am aware that this interpretation reverses the grim picture of these people that is usually supplied by critics but that is because I am convinced that their examination of the Lost Generation has never been anything but superficial. They saw the triumph of nothingness but did not ask themselves what was the quality of the response. Nor do I pretend that this Generation had entered a state of grace. I am simply claiming that their solution was as valid as the hybrid of more respectable people and also that their subconscious harboured fewer furies than many a suburban dweller's.

I am willing to call their attitude one of despair

but not of defeat, which the word usually implies. They had found an answer to despair and transformed it into something dead and innocuous. (The Profile writer is correct when he notices the courage and the virility.) Despair does not really exist when its power is not acknowledged. I prefer to call the state one of accepted despair. Like an insult, it is reduced to nothing when it is taken without umbrage.

I would like to examine the critical method of those who accuse Hemingway's characters (and Hemingway himself is always assumed) of critical despair. A few instances will suffice. The Russian J. Kashkeen naturally applies the Marxist criterion. Hemingway is the victim of his own individualist outlook and, travelling by the road to perdition familiar to all Marxist critics, arrives at nada. His 'sight is limited by the blinders of sceptical individualism. Life is too complicated and full of deceit. The romance of war has been deceit, it is on deceit that the renown of most writers rests.'[1] This could only be a revealing comment if Hemingway were quite a different person from the one he is. He has always pricked the romance-balloon of war and he shows little respect for many literary reputations. When he sees these deceits, despite his blinders, he is taking the first step towards renovation. He was not introducing a climate of nada, it had already arrived. Kashkeen then cunningly says, 'There is despair in the feeling of impending doom, and morbidity in the foretaste of the imminent loss of all that was dear.'

[1] 'A Tragedy of Craftsmanship', from *Ernest Hemingway: the Man and his Work*, ed. J. McCaffery.

Cunningly, because there is a barely noticeable trans-
ference from character to author. The term despair
is again used dishonestly. The despair is accepted,
and 'impending doom' is a nonsensical idiom to apply
to Hemingway's world. There was never a literature
with less sense of doom. The doom is supplied by the
reader. The confusion arises because Hemingway was
at that time one of the few who had stepped across
the chasm. He resembles Leonardo in his rôle as
pioneer in a new territory of psychic experience.[1] I,
cannot help suspecting that Hemingway's real fault,
so far as Kashkeen was concerned, lay in his refusal
to join the Communist Party. Had he done that
Kashkeen would have hailed the very work he had
depreciated as a herald of the new literature that was
to lay bare the rottenness of capitalist society. (Incidentally, Hemingway took a sly revenge on this critic
by naming Robert Jordan's predecessor as dynamiter
Kashkin, a man who could not control his fear. 'I
think he was very tired and nervous and he imagined
ugly things.')

Another critic who drew attention to Hemingway's individualism, but in a far more realistic way,
was Maxwell Geismar. His view is interesting because
it echoes Gertrude Stein's Rotarian give. Geismar
claims that Hemingway's individualism (which is

[1] In self-defence I have compared Hemingway to Froissart
and now to Leonardo. There is a type of critic who will
get endless fun out of these comparisons unless I forestall
him. The comparisons only hold good in very limited
fields – in the case of Froissart as chronicler, in the case of
Leonardo as pioneer.

undeniable) is an extension of the American business
man's commercial individualism as portrayed earlier
by Ring Lardner.

> The 'I' which for so many years was the single star to
> guide Hemingway over foreign boulevards and African
> jungles is not, after all, very different from the self-
> absorption of the typical man of America's boom era.
> The artistic metier was simply replacing the economic.
> In the method of his renunciation Hemingway bears
> the sign of the society he is renouncing. Disowning his
> social and his human obligations in favour of 'art',
> Hemingway was in the end very close to the business
> man of the twenties who spoke in similar terms of his
> own commercial achievement.[1]

The dilemma in which Hemingway found himself goes something like this. He saw the collapse of
all but material values and he saw the calm acceptance of this collapse. There was no despair as we
know it. He realised that there was something more
that he wanted from life. The myth-seeking part of
him gave him no rest. But his equipment was entirely
American. He had been formed by a commercial
society which for a period had really believed in salvation through the machine and had willingly and in
good faith broken with the inefficient past. He wished
to recover the unknown quantity (it was really a
quality) which would have enriched life but his tools
were those of a high-pressure salesman. We get occasional glimpses of an impulse towards Catholicism,
with the suspicion that this body of rejected wisdom
may after all contain valuable clues. *The Torrents of*

[1] *Writers in Crisis*, by Maxwell Geismar.

Spring is really an account of this conflict. It is correct
to stress the Americanism of Hemingway but it
should not be forgotten that his Americanism is set
to work in a different field from that of the majority
of his compatriots. He is rather like a Hot Gospeller
who preaches Christianity through athletic prowess.
And this is where we can draw a distinction between
Hemingway and, let us say, Jake Barnes. Jake has
ceased to care – except for the outcrops. Hemingway
cares, but he does his best to hide it because he has
a conventional conception of conduct which is reluctant to betray his innermost feelings. Jake Barnes is
Hemingway in experience and outer reaction; Hemingway nurses his own spiritual misgivings and denies
them entirely to Jake.

An amusing instance of this personal conflict is
to be found, unless I am making a big mistake, in
Hemingway's Preface to Lee Samuels' *Checklist* of
his works. Here he writes rather in the manner of a
tired business man giving us the embittered benefit
of his life's 'philosophy'. (In these accounts men are
either entirely good at heart or entirely wicked.)
Writing of Samuels' work in assembling the list he
says, 'It is such a disinterested action that it is impressive to the point of being almost incredible in
these times.' This sounds like the cynicism which is
so fashionable these days. It is the kind of judgment
one naturally expects from Big Game Hunter,
aficionado, fisherman and soldier. Having read most
of Hemingway's published work I doubt if he means
a word of what he says here. He is under the compulsion to remain at the heart of the culture he really

despises. He wishes to impress them on their own ground. I would say that Hemingway has faith not in all people but in a great many people.

One can experience despair, and with it frustration and cynicism, in three ways. The familiar impact is when one's faith is broken and life is rendered almost insupportable by the realisation of helplessness. The accepted despair of the Lost Generation consists of acquiescence and a determination to ask for little and avoid the risk of disappointment. The third is a development from one or other of these two – an attempt to restore or rebuild, to be reborn in theological and psychoanalytical terms. Hemingway has worked through to this position. He has left Jake Barnes behind and at the same time is not content to be a professional pessimist. But he is not only a man, he is a special kind of man, an artist. 'The artist, I believe, is more primitive, as well as more civilised, than his contemporaries; his experience is deeper than civilisation, and he only uses the phenomena of his civilisation in expressing it.'[1] He has dug deep and shown us what he has seen, but more than any other writer of the first rank he has used the phenomena of his civilisation in expressing it.

Every acceptance implies a rejection. The face of despair can only be worn if it rejects the living values; its reality demands them and fails to find them. There are three major rejections at the heart of Hemingway's work, though the emphasis varies with his development: the animal rejection of all

[1] T. S. Eliot, review of *Tarr*, by Wyndham Lewis, in *The Egoist*.

but the merely biological plane of living, the sophisticated rejection of all responsibility except that of
self-indulgence and having a good time, and the
philosophic or heroic rejection of letting the world
go its way and standing for personal ties alone. They
are illustrated in the first three novels. The biological
plane of living is represented by Harry Morgan, the
evasion of responsibility by Jake Barnes, the elevation of personal ties by Frederick Henry. The only
one of these who experiences the agony of classical
despair is Henry, and that is because he is immature.
We see the change taking place. With the help of
critical automatism it is simple to classify writers into
accepters and rejecters. For instance, Vance Bourjaily
in his novel *The End of My Life* enables three friends
to draw up two rival football teams composed of
writers and thinkers, the Yes team and the No team.
Hemingway is in the latter. Yet Harry Morgan
affirmed courage, Frederick Henry love and Jake
Barnes the will to survival, even a limited happiness.
(Not that I disapprove of the method, providing that
it is recognised it proves nothing final, for it was in
precisely this way that I discovered that Gower was
a remarkably solid full back and that Wyndham
Lewis is still one of the best bats in the country.)

I have tried to show by this digression that Hemingway is not one of his own characters, that he
understands their rejections because he has at one
time or another shared them (it is his method as
novelist to do so) and that he has passed beyond them.
To return to Maxwell Geismar's thesis, the claim
is made that no other writer has found life so com-

pletely vain, that he does not understand the destructive impulses underlying humanity's actions, and he *therefore* declares the world has no problems and no meaning. The italicised word betrays the falseness of the logic. It is true that you will not find in his work the awareness of myth and its relation to human action that you will find in, say, T. S. Eliot. But Hemingway is by no means the first writer whose understanding has lacked this awareness yet has been significant in mythical terms. He may not formally understand the destructive impulses yet his instinctive understanding is acute. To speak of 'the emptiness which covers the frustration of the writer who is unable to cope with his true material' is to deny the existence of Hemingway as an artist. The function of the artist is to impose a pattern on his experience, not to search it for motives and impulses. The kind of literature that Geismar appears to want is fairly prolific these days, particularly in America, and it is universally unsatisfying. To attribute every action to the Oedipus complex or homosexual desires or mother fixation is not only boring but it is almost certainly untrue. Hemingway's conception of impulse is something that can be discovered if we take the trouble and if we do not attempt to comfine it to a few categories rescued from classical mythology. I would not venture to set my views against Jung's – there are plenty of other people doing that already and anyway I'd rather defend Jung against the literary Jungians. But it is possible that the old myths do not account for every type of action, especially after the lapse of centuries during which the psyche may have been modified in a way corresponding to the modification of the body. (For instance, it may be that the pursuit of wealth is a more powerful motive these days than it was: in the major plays of Sophocles there is only one reference to it and three more in the fragments. What would be the result of such a count in the works of, let us say, Shaw?)

I often wish it were possible to write all sections of a book simultaneously. A book is an artificial thing and it is incapable of reproducing the vitality of thought, which is multidimensional. As it is, I must deal with the myth-making aspect of Hemingway separately. In this chapter I have tried to describe his treatment of the despair so prevalent in our civilisation. Eliot has done it also. But there is a vast difference between poetry and the novel. Poetry is recognised as a fit vehicle for discussion and reflection, the novel is not. Hemingway enters the world of Prufrock, Sweeney and Gerontion and brings back miniatures of their emptiness and frustration. Frederick Henry explaining to the priest that we never do the things we want to do, that even when we wish to behave decently something malignant in our psyche propels us in the opposite direction; the girl in 'Hills Like White Elephants' putting the old complaint of gall and wormwood into modern forms: 'Everything tastes like liquorice. Especially all the things you've waited so long for, like absinthe'; Rinaldi finding the same lack of savour in everything except two – and 'one is bad for my work and the other is over in half an hour or fifteen minutes'; Robert Jordan realising that he had been manoeuvred into such a position by the society he could not escape that life had ceased to consist of anything more than today, tonight and tomorrow.

Eliot has put all these failures into his poetry. 'His laughter tinkled among the teacups.' 'I stiffen in a rented house.' 'Lonely men in shirtsleeves leaning out of windows.' They all share the same word of decay and despair. Eliot, being a poet, could relate his moderns to Agamemnon and Antony. Hemingway, being a novelist, could not.

* * * * *

The Torrents of Spring is something quite apart from the rest of Hemingway's output. It is a deliberate piece of myth-making. American civilisation is cracking up. It narrows down to pump-making, with razor-blades as a sideline. The rest is just holes in the heart. Men wandering the cold countryside, looking for work, wondering how to fill the great void of life. Women wondering how they can hold their men, trying desperately to win their love with hopeless tactics on the edge of living. Spring threatens to come but it does not come. The countryside remains frozen, men remain empty. Industry is frightened.

Then a naked Indian woman walks into a beanery. Yogi Johnson suddenly realises what is lacking, suddenly discovers the remedy for living death. He casts off his clothes and follows the woman. This is the only possible alternative to Paris. The American will never learn to live like the Parisian. His only hope is to recivilise himself in the pattern of the true indigenous American. The chinook wind starts to blow, the snow to melt, and Yogi to want a woman again.

This could never be a popular book. That possibility exists for all his other books but not for this. It is unusual, it is facetious (this word is used to denote high spirits, which are tabu), and it requires a degree of receptivity from the reader that is rarely forthcoming. It will remain as a curiosity, especially as the great literary ferment of the 'twenties and 'thirties is dying down and respectability and conformability are becoming literary values again. But nothing Hemingway has done demonstrates so clearly his detestation of our contemporary shackles. It may be his most important book when there is an educated public.

CHAPTER IX

MYTH-MAKING

A

I HAVE said that we can discover the myth in Hemingway's work so long as we approach it in the right spirit and without an *a priori* conviction that it does not exist. We can, for instance, regard Jake Barnes as an incarnation of the Fisher King awaiting the question. Both were sexually impotent. The probability that Hemingway had never read the Grail Legend and thus would be unaware of the correspondence would not destroy the moral significance of *Fiesta*, which is what critics like Geismar imply. But there is an important difference between the two, and it is this difference that makes *Fiesta* more than a mere re-statement of an old myth in modern terms. The impotence of the Fisher King was curable but there was no question and no operation that could have cured Jake. If we like we can read into this Hemingway's conviction at that time that the condition of our society was beyond remedy.

Another. There is a suggestion that on the point of death Harry Morgan is spiritually reborn but it is too late for anything he can do in this world. His groping towards a sense of community, if only in opposition, could be regarded as the first faltering step, a very imperfect one, towards a sense of union with the life-principle itself (the most universal myth of all). The rites of the early mystery cults were very severe and sometimes cost the initiate his reason. Morgan lost his life. No doubt this is far-fetched. Morgan was a scoundrel. But he is partially redeemed by qualities that place him on a level superior to most of the other characters in the novel.

But a myth can be re-enacted without the assurance that its protagonists will transcend themselves. Hemingway's characters are not 'transformed' in Jung's meaning of the term, i.e. having reached a dead end in the field of conscious adaptation to external experience without achieving any sense of fulfilment, they are unable to effect a radical change in themselves. They are mostly unaware of their loss of communion with any life-giving source. They probably go to their deaths in the manner of Aegisthus, unrepentant and even unaware of the need for repentance.

The charge against Hemingway is that the universal myths of the past are lost to him. It is the very charge that Eliot made against our whole civilisation in *The Waste Land* when he calls the myths of the ancient world 'a heap of broken images'. But in his humility Eliot knows that he himself is part of that culture and shares its responsibilities. Hemingway illustrates the broken images and his awareness or unawareness of their significance is a matter of no importance. We should not require a novelist to be a priest.

The enormous volume of knowledge with which a modern critic has to grapple is no doubt partly responsible for the partiality of so much modern criticism. While Hemingway can rightly (though

irrelevantly) be accused of ignoring the kind of mythology the Jungians have found so rewarding, there
is another department of myth, still alive in a vital
ritual, in which Hemingway is saturated. One of the
fairest of all the Hemingway critics, Malcolm Cowley, tells me that in his opinion the most important
feature of Hemingway's work is 'his pre-Christian and
pre-civilised instinct for myth and ritual'.[1] Cowley
examined this instinct in his introduction to *The
Viking Portable Hemingway*. It is typical of Hemingway that he should be attracted by an ancient
myth that is still enacted. It is also typical of many
people who have not his lust for the living moment
that they should be sceptical of a myth's value whose
ritual has persisted into the present. They would
rather discuss man's victory over the bestial principle
by reference to the exploits of Theseus than to those
of Juan Belmonte. Anticipating their conclusions,
they assume that the ritual of the bullfight is a debase-
ment of one that was once meaningful. They would
assert that the spectator at the bullfight is as divorced
from the true sources of life as an Arsenal supporter.
But there is the same old twist to the argument – is
Hemingway's participation in the ritual to be depreciated because the yelling crowd has been divorced
from the rite's vital sources?

Hemingway does in fact give us plenty of evidence that the bullfight is not merely a spectacle to
him. It is in his approach to the bullfight that he

[1] And not only myth and ritual. Behind the civilised façade
in *The Torrents of Spring* Scripps hears continually the
war-whoops of the Indians and the laughter of the Negroes.

tends to become mystical – and, strangely, he is attacked for it. To begin with, he recognises the pre-Christian element in the Spanish consciousness–or Robert Jordan does, and Hemingway could scarcely describe an attitude that he does not know himself. He senses a difference in the Spaniard's approach to killing, and it is very similar to what Arturo Barea said. Barea claimed that the Spaniard does not kill in cold blood and that he requires an enemy that is capable of killing him. Killing in a modern war is a business, performed without any kind of exaltation.

> Yes, Robert Jordan thought. We do it coldly but they do not, nor ever have. It is their extra sacrament. Their old one that they had before the new religion came from the far end of the Mediterranean, the one they have never abandoned but only suppressed and hidden to bring it out again in wars and inquisitions. They are the people of the Auto-da-Fé; the act of faith.

This sense of the bullfight being pre-Christian is not a mere solitary flash. On the first page of *Death in the Afternoon* he supposes that, 'from a modern moral point of view, that is, a Christian point of view, the whole bullfight is indefensible'. Max Eastman reminds us that 'until Christians thought up the sickly idea of worshipping a lamb, this noble creature symbolised the beauty of divine power in a good half of the great religions of the earth'.[1] There is, then, a throwback to an early civilisational stage which implies a challenge to the Christian ethic. The killing of the bull can be interpreted as the killing of a god

[1] From *Art and the Life of Action.*

and the assimilation of his great power. Or if we omit the divinity, it is the killing of a magnificent and powerful beast with the consequent proof of man's superiority. The bull is a symbol of strength, always appealing to Hemingway, and it could be identified in certain respects with the simplest of all the Greek myth-heroes, Hercules. Only man triumphs over him. Applying the usual ambivalence inherent in mythology, the Hercules element in man is revealed by his victory over the bull.

Then there is the purely religious interpretation, in which we see the bullfighter as a sacrificial priest, officiating in a religion where bulls are offered as substitutes for men. 'It was Hemingway's misfortune that the war failed to teach him how men died, so he had to investigate the artifice of how men have continued to kill and not be killed. Only the behaviour of a man in the face of sure death seems to convince him of his ability to live.'[1] As we have seen, it was a way of asserting his superiority to death and his release from the fear of death. The bullfighter-priest offered the bull to the gods and won a renewed lease of life. Hemingway himself says there are three ways of killing a bull: as a vocational killer, as a butcher (i.e. professional) and as a priest.

I am not saying which of these interpretations, if any, is correct. I merely record them because they have all been advanced by different commentators. They may all be nonsense. The critic's craft often leads him beyond the sphere of acceptable interpre-

[1] Lincoln Kirstein, 'The Canon of Death', from *Ernest Hemingway: the Man and his Work*, ed. J. McCaffery.

tation, usually through the neglect of aspects which do not harmonise with a theory or temperament. My main purpose here is to show that Hemingway gets more than mere spectatorial sensations out of a bull-fight and that it is very easy indeed to discern the presence of a mythos in his work if we feel the need for it. By mythos I mean the symbolic reflection of a primitive consciousness.

Let me illustrate the emotion that Hemingway feels during a well-conducted bullfight in his own words.

> The *faena* that takes a man out of himself and makes him feel immortal while it is proceeding, that gives him an ecstasy that is, while momentary, as profound as any religious ecstasy; moving all the people in the ring together and increasing in emotional intensity as it proceeds, carrying the bullfighter with it, he playing on the crowd through the bull and being moved as it responds in a growing ecstasy of ordered, formal, passionate, increasing disregard for death that leaves you, when it is over, and the death administered to the animal that has made it possible, as empty, as changed and as sad as any major emotion will leave you.[1]

The emphasis is constantly on emotion and ecstasy. The linking of ecstasy with the terms 'ordered, formal, passionate' is reminiscent of the best poetry. The above description could probably have been applied, with minor changes of reference, to the rites of the classical mysteries. The dominant sense, lying behind the shared ecstasy and emotion, is one of communion. The devotees must have approached Dionysos in some such way.

[1] *Death in the Afternoon.*

171

The true bullfighter must be a dedicated killer. He must be a man for whom killing is not a crime, as in secular life, but a high office, as in all primitive religions. He must kill because he believes killing is the price paid for the renewal of life.

> A great killer must love to kill; unless he feels it is the best thing he can do, unless he is conscious of its dignity and feels that it is his own reward, he will be incapable of the abnegation that is necessary in real killing. The truly great killer must have a sense of honour and a sense of glory far beyond that of the ordinary bull-fighter. In other words he must be a simpler man... he must have a spiritual enjoyment of the moment of killing.

He fights a duel with death and death's presence is proved by the bodies of the horses lying in the sand. Overcoming death, 'he gives the feeling of his immortality, and, as you watch it, it becomes yours'. Hemingway sees this momentarily superhuman priest conducting a sacramental drama conventionally divided into three acts: trial, sentence, execution. It is a pre-Christian mystery play.

Death in the Afternoon is his only book in which the mystical element is intrusive. Because of it we know that the other books are not mere accounts of situation and sensation, but that they are cloaked with the material garments of a civilisation that has forgotten myth and rejected the bullfight. The nearest approach to uncloaking is to be found in the character of Harry Morgan, whom Edmund Wilson sees as a hybrid, half Hemingway legendary figure, half nature (fertility) myth hero. He is the modern

Hercules, the man whose virtue lies in his strength and courage. But Hercules still lives under the guise of Popeye and Superman. These are the great modern myth heroes and Hemingway recognises them. When he leaves Spain he leaves the religious atmosphere behind as well. If his nature demands the mythical element he finds it ready to hand. The hero of the people is Harry Morgan. This is what he sees.

Apart from love, the only mystery the Colonel of *Across the River* believed in was the 'occasional bravery of man'. It is the only one that is applauded today. Again, that is what Hemingway found.

B

'Being essentially the instrument for his work, he (the great artist) is subordinate to it, and we have no reason for expecting him to interpret it for us. He has done the best that in him lies by giving it form, and he must leave interpretation to others and to the future. A great work of art is like a dream. ... it does not explain itself and is never unequivocal. A dream never says: "you ought," or: "This is the truth". It presents an image... To grasp its meaning, we must allow it to shape us as it once shaped the artist. Then we understand the nature of the experience.'

C. G. Jung, *Modern Man in Search of a Soul.*

C

But it may be that the author makes his own legend. A man does not choose to make a legend. It

173

is made by the force in him and he is controlled by the force. Later, when he enjoys the reputation his legend gives him, he may reinforce it consciously and intensively. In time a legend, which is local and tribal, may become a myth. Hemingway is the centre of a legend that is better known than his work. This is always true when it happens because most people find it easier to memorise impressive situations than to survive the imaginative effort of mentally assimilating a work of art.

For a legendary figure certain qualities must be abstracted and emphasised at the expense of others. In Hemingway's case they are courage, ruthlessness, toughness, sporting skill, lack of emotion and other qualities all exhibiting a mixture of recklessness and psychological hardness. The first stage of abstraction is done by reader and spectator, the second and more dangerous one by the author himself. Hemingway's courage is of the compulsive type, as in the example given by John Groth, quoted in a previous chapter. Knowing what we do of Hemingway, it is unlikely that he continued to sit at table eating his meal when the windows came in and the others flung themselves on the floor because he felt no fear; it was his determination to combat his fear.

There is no lack of stories illustrating the legendary qualities I have listed. For instance, hardness: meeting an English writer in Paris with his wife during the Spanish War he said to him, 'Take her to Spain and show her the corpses. That'll make a new woman of her'. Or controlled emotion: while having breakfast in a Madrid hotel in 1936 Hemingway was asserting the impossibility of the Fascist guns hitting the hotel, when there was an explosion and the ceiling fell on the table. With a smile Hemingway said, 'That's the way it goes, gentlemen', almost as though it had proved his point. Or the well-known story illustrating his wordly common sense: Scott Fitzgerald saying to him, 'You know, Ernest, the rich are different from us', and Hemingway answering, 'Yes, they have more money'. This takes us back to an earlier phase in the legend, the Paris of the twenties with endless and aimless drinking and uninhibited sex. But this has been overgrown, the follies forgotten under the weight of the mature will. Finally, the sporting aspect: 1935, when he won the fishing tournament at Bimini and offered $ 200 to anyone who could stay four rounds with him in the ring, but he beat them all, and then boxed exhibition rounds with Tom Heeney, the British heavyweight champion. People who know him swear the truth of the stories that make up the legend. There seems little doubt that Hemingway could have become a first-class boxer.

Edmund Wilson claims that the legend has interfered with the art, and instances *Green Hills of Africa* which falls between 'the two genres of personal exhibitionism and fiction'.[1] The legend was built up steadily through the 'thirties and on up to the present until, according to Wilson, he began to exploit his personality for profit.

He turns up delivering Hemingway monologues in

[1] *The Wound and the Bow.*

wellpaying and trashy magazines; and the Hemingway of these loose disquisitions, arrogant, belligerent and boastful, is certainly the worst-invented character to be found in the author's work. If he is obnoxious, the effect is somewhat mitigated by the fact that he is intrinsically incredible.

The incredibility is a matter of personal taste and imagination and, presumably, knowledge. The only incredible thing to me is that anything else should be considered incredible in a world that still refuses to adjust itself to theological and scientific dogmas. All I feel it necessary to say at this point is that either Hemingway does or he wishes to live his own work. It is not normally considered necessary for artistic creation. The artist's feeling can steal into a person and extract his essence. But Hemingway has always believed in identification rather than empathy.

We are still within the legend's development, though probably near its end, and so it is impossible to make a final judgment. *Across the River* shows signs of the legend going sour. But there are a few comments which may throw an interim light on the subject. Homer and Havelock did not think of posterity. Later poets, makars and especially writers, impressed by the durability of parchment and paper, thought of it increasingly. The surge of egoism which occurred at the time of the renaissance emphasised the trend. The hope that a small section of their work might 'live' was born and grew. When they spoke of work as living they meant something quite different from people living – they meant living for ever, immortality, which they could not hope for themselves. Once you have considered the possibility of posterity reading your work you will also consider, from your knowledge of human curiosity, the certainly that they will want to know something of you, the author. And so we have the pressures to build up a legend, the conscious attempt to create a character who lives like his work, a tough, virile Hemingway who will smack his critics down, a jesting Shaw who will never give a direct answer.

This view may be odious because of its basis in automatism but it is no more automatic than a psychoanalytic theory. A writer is subject to the condition of his craft. Without a public his work does not exist. He is often temped to feel that without a public *he* may not exist. He is tethered to his work. Many critics have told him that Madame Bovary is greater than Flaubert.

CHAPTER X

CULTURE AND TRADITION

THE trouble started when Aldous Huxley objected to a passage in *Farewell to Arms* where a reference is made to 'the bitter nail holes' of Mantegna's Christ.[1] Huxley adds that Hemingway, appalled by this excursion into the world of Culture, hurries on to speak once more of Lower Things.

First of all, it must be admitted that in the early work of Hemingway there is an almost complete lack of reference to those parts of our culture which were formerly regarded as essential framework for any serious writer, such as E. M. Forster and Henry James. Secondly, it must also be admitted that Hemingway's defence is a good one. He wants to know why he should force his characters to speak of things which they never mention in normal conversation – in other words, that Huxley was criticising the cultural level not of Hemingway but of his characters. If there was a further criticism, that Hemingway had no right to deal in Calibans only Hemingway politely told him to mind his own business (which happened to be with Calibans educated into Ariels).

> If the people the writer is making talk of old misters; of music; of modern painting; of letters or of science then they should talk of those subjects in the novel. If they do not talk of those subjects and the writer makes them talk of them he is a faker, and if he talks about them himself to show how much he knows then he is show-

---

[1] 'Foreheads Villainous Low'.

ing off. No matter how good a phrase or simile he may have if he puts it in when it is not absolutely necessary and irreplaceable he is spoiling his work for egotism.[1]

The dispossessed people of whom Hemingway was writing had had no artistic training. If Catherine Barkley went to an English Secondary School she could not possibly have understood even the meaning of art, yet alone been able to discuss it intelligently in detail – unless she had possessed abnormal intellectual curiosity, of which there is no evidence. Here are she and Henry 'discussing' art in the rather ashamed way people adopt when they are talking about things of which they are entirely ignorant and which in any case are 'unnecessary' and therefore 'queer'.

> 'Do you know anything about art?'
> 'Rubens', said Catherine.
> 'Large and fat', I said.
> 'Titian', Catherine said.
> 'Titian-haired', I said. 'How about Mantegna?'
> 'Don't ask hard ones', Catherine said.

And then we get the nail-holes. Probably pathetic but pathetically true. The fact that Henry had been an architectural student is of no relevance – it is not difficult to find English Honours men who hate and are also afraid of literature. Expecting Hemingway to make his people discuss art in terms of form and tone is like expecting him to explain the mythical significance of Cohn.

I know nothing firsthand of American education

[1] *Death in the Afternoon.*

but it is probably not superior in this respect. We get a glimpse of the academic awe in which certain writers are held, a typical product of our educational methods. Nick and Bill are trying to get their authors in racing order and are stumped because Chesterton and Walpole are both classics, but they don't know exactly *how* classical they are. ('Three Day Blow'.) These judgments are categorical like the horse-power of an engine. And I have heard with my own ears a high-up education officer saying he supposed *The Blue Lagoon* is a classic.

The truth is, the culture of the past is an enigma to most people in the present. If it seems to them to be dull, difficult to understand, remote in feeling and rather austere the odds are it is classical. All marble busts looked alike to Frederick Henry. He used to look at them in the office of Catherine's hospital and he remembered many more in Genoa. 'But they were all uniformly classical. You could not tell anything about them.' A straightforward admission that the past was dead and could not speak to us over the gap of time. We must not be too hasty in assuming that these young men and women had deliberately turned their backs on the old European heritage, as it is proudly called. If they had done that it would have been because they had something to put in its place. For some reason or other (and I have a sneaking feeling that it was that lamentable failure, universal education) they had lost the language.[1]

[1] But in *The Torrents of Spring* he writes of 'Europeans, members of a worn-out civilisation world-weary from the war'.

Hemingway does not deal specifically nor usually with what is termed the proletariat: in its original meaning the factory-working population, in looser usage the working class. But in spiritual terms he is almost entirely concerned with that section of the population that lies below the level of 'Western Culture', consisting of an assimilation of Shakespeare, Donne, Dryden, Gray, Wordsworth, Keats, Browning, Yeats and Eliot. (It must be understood that I use these names symbolically.) Most Europeans have always been below this level in its academic significance but they have regarded it as a level worthy of attainment. Proportionately the numbers below, unaware and uncaring, have risen steeply since they were compelled to read trash and to be bored with 'classics'. Hemingway writes of the great majority who enjoy *Kitsch* and comprise the *Biedermeierkultur,* neither of which terms they have ever encountered. They might well be astonished, like M. Jourdain. D. S. Savage, writing in *Focus*, regards the work of Hemingway as 'a special form of that which might be termed the *proletarianisation* of literature: the adaptation of the technical artistic conscience to the sub-average human consciousness'.[1]

Mario Praz has commented on Hemingway's immense popularity and influence in Italy, particularly among the younger generation of writers. (Hemingway has reciprocated by awarding the Premio Hemingway for what he considers the best Italian work of fiction submitted during the year.) Emilio

[1] D. S. Savage, 'Ernest Hemingway, *Focus* 2', ed. B. Rajan and Andrew Pearse.

Cecchi says he has 'hit upon a literature which has nothing to do with literature, which is not spoiled or weakened by literature'. This popularity is of more value in our assessment of Hemingway than a whole symposium of individual judgments. The process of proletarianisation has been more rapid in Italy since the war than in any other European country. I do not refer to the actual social and industrial situation but to the tone of modern Italian art and thought. The Italian film, for instance, is steeped in the robustness and virility of an ethos that insists on the glorification of poverty, or rather the human qualities that thrive in it, not for political but for artistic ends. The beauty of squalor is the new Italian message. It differs from the British proletarian literature of the 'thirties because it does manage to trick beauty out of its antitheses. And now we have a literature that is no literature, that acknowledges no sacred names, that will sweep d'Annunzio and Manzoni into the dustbin along with the Renaissance glories which woo the tourist and of which the native Italian is sick and tired.

In his frequent (yes, frequent!) references to the great names of art Hemingway usually manages to point a contrast between them and the sordid, ignorant present. One of the main rôles of the great work of the past is to stand up as mute witnesses of something that has been lost, like mysterious monoliths in a desert. In *The Fifth Column* Dorothy and Philip listen to the Chopin *Mazurka in C Minor, opus* 33, *No.* 4. As accompaniment there is the occasional whoosh of a shell overhead, followed by the explosion and the clattering of brick and glass. There is no electricity and they can only see each other by the light from the glow of an electric heater.

I believe that Hemingway is genuinely impressed by much of the great work of the past. I also believe he has been worried by some of the criticisms of his anticulture and sometimes his late work has been distorted by those very attempts to inject culture that he has said are a fake. But I would prefer to discuss the reactions of his characters (or people as he prefers to call them) and leave identification to others. Certainly there is or was a great deal of Hemingway in Lieutenant Henry and perhaps Henry's bewilderment and at times bitterness in the face of the traditional culture of the past was also Hemingway's. When Henry was waiting for Catherine at her hospital he looked at the frescoes on the wall. 'The frescoes were not bad. Any frescoes were good when they started to peel and flake off.' This is a very nice example of controlled bitterness, but it is difficult to know how to interpret it. Is it the sub-man's delight in seeing the things he cannot appreciate falling to pieces? Or is it an ironical reflection on a condition of society in which the art and skill of the past have been debased to a decoration of a war that is destroying all it stands for?

Whatever the answer, I have no doubt that Hemingway is intensely suspicious of the closed world of culture, taste and refinement into which he has never entered. It is so very possible that we are being cheated, that the impressive apparatus of dealers, critics, buyers, glossy magazine editors and connoisseurs may in reality be a racket thriving on trivialities, shams and other people's ignorance. In *Death in the Afternoon* he notes how disappointed the tourists are when they visit the Prado and find it simply arranged and well-lighted. This is not what they have learnt to expect from their experience of the gloom and chaos of Italian galleries.

> Great art should have great frames and needs either red plush or bad lighting to back it up. It is as though after having known of certain things only through reading pornographic literature the tourist should be introduced to an attractive woman quite unclothed, with no draperies, no concealments and no conversation and only the plainest of beds. He would probably want a book to aid him or at least a few properties or suggestions.

He draws attention to the way in which critics are liable to lose all sense of proportion when they are involved in a new enthusiasm. He cites Julius Meier-Graefe who went to Spain because he wanted to have 'publishable ecstasies' about Goya and Velasquez but stayed to write a book proving how superior Greco was to both. He did it by showing that Greco's crucifixion of Christ was superior to the others', but as Greco was the only one of the three who was interested in the subject there was no ground for comparison. In other words, an artistic furore is often worked up around a particular artist at the expense of others in a field where he has no opposition – and all other fields are neglected. By confining this study to the artistic treatment of the bullring I could prove Hemingway the greatest writer of all time, which I don't, being a very cautious man. I could also make Hemingway look a third-rate hack in the presence of, say, Charles Williams.

In this kind of direct, common-sense criticism Hemingway is a master. One benefit derived from his preoccupation with the outer world is his sense of balance when considering all things that have to be seen clean and straight. When he enters the mystical field he does tend to become unbalanced, as Eastman has shown. But because he is something more than a common man he can see how easily the common man is tricked. He is constantly on his guard. He is on his guard against those things with which he is not familiar, the marbles and the frescoes. But when there is nothing inserted between his own judgment and the object, when he does not have to rely on the possibly prejudiced opinion of a curator or connoisseur, he can be as natural and appreciative as any man who is capable of feeling. Not easily, of course. The mask will not allow easy emotion. But, as someone has anticipated me in saying, love will break down the stiff barrier of conventional behaviour. Frederick Henry can even quote poetry, and without any sense of shame.

> The waiter came and took away the things. After a while we were very still and we could hear the rain. Down below on the street a motor car honked.
>   'And always at my back I hear
>   Time's winged chariot hurrying near'
> I said.
>   'I know that poem', Catherine said. 'It's by Marvell. But it's about a girl who wouldn't live with a man'.

But love is not the only crisis that will do it. Remembered lines of poetry float in our unconscious like myths, ready to surface and give their assistance to the task of adaption to awkward reality. Even Wilson, the white hunter, was affected. Normally he spoke only of his craft plus the useful counters of small talk that were really part of his craft. Yet when he saw Macomber conquering his fear and realised, without thinking it, that he had witnessed a purgation, the words came to his lips uncalled.

> 'That's it', said Wilson. 'Worst one can do is kill you. How does it go? Shakespeare. Damned good. See if I can remember. Oh, damned good. Used to quote it to myself at one time. Let's see. "By my troth, I care not; a man can die but once; we owe God a death, and let it go which way it will he that dies this year is quiet for the next." Damned fine, eh?'
> He was very embarrassed, having brought out this thing he had lived by...

He was embarrassed but Henry and Catherine Barkley were not. They had been entirely involved in the emotion that stirred them, while he had been a spectator and only partly affected by the emotion's backwash.

It is difficult, in view of some of Hemingway's descriptive passages, to understand how anyone could ever accuse him of anticulture. They mean, of course, the culture of the past but that is an easier thing to acquire than a truly contemporary culture. A person of true contemporary culture will see the shams in past culture immediately. Contemporary culture is at the end of a long tradition. It is a vantage point from which the foregoing can be seen without hindrance. Each of us is born to the tradition; it is up to us whether we assimilate it or not. But assimilation is a matter of tone, not of names. There is many ignorant Catholic who contains Dante within him without having read a line of the Divine Comedy. Our present consciousness has been partly formed by Dostoievsky but only a minority have read him. Even Sidney Dobell did not live in vain. We must ask ourselves whether Hemingway could possibly have written down his battlescapes if the way had not been prepared for him. Such scenes and, for instance, his description of Aranjuez in *Death in the Afternoon* ('Velasquez to the edge and then straight Goya to the bullring') come not only from the eyes of a Hemingway but also from those of a long line of artists from Brueghel to Paul Nash.

The gap between the old traditions and new contemporary feeling does not escape his comment.

> The individual, the great artist when he comes, uses everything that has been discovered or known about his art up to that point, being able to accept or reject in a time so short it seems that the knowledge was born with him, rather than that he takes instantly what it takes the ordinary man a lifetime to know, and then the great artist goes beyond what has been done or known and makes something of his own. But there is sometimes a long time between great ones and those that have known the former great ones rarely recognise the new ones when they come. They want the old, the way it was that they remember it. But the others, the contemporaries, recognise the new great ones because

of their ability to know so quickly, and finally even the ones who remember the old do. They are excused from, not recognising at once because they, in the period of waiting, see so many false ones that they become so cautious that they cannot trust their feelings; only their memory. Memory, of course, is never true.[1]

The point is well made. It is not an easy matter, cultivating a tradition so that it grows straight and true and does not become constantly tangled with its own past. The difficulties are increasing for fewer people share in the tradition and are assisted in their continual function of erosion by those who have shared but stopped dead. When the moral collapse came after the first war it was Hemingway who salvaged a few values out of the wreckage. Others, writing at though there had been no collapse, committed artistic suicide. The greatness of *Farewell to Arms* lies in its dramatisation of the conflict between struggling values and chaos. There is love in this novel, fighting hard, there is even religion. You will not find a surrender nor a fake pretence that the old values are still in the best of health, even if confined to an ivory tower or a country parsonage.

In one of his stories there is clear evidence that at least one of the traditional values finds a champion in the author – or at least, the 'I' figure. A bull fighter's mother had been buried for five years. At the end of the period he received a notice of renewal, demanding twenty dollars for perpetual burial. Although he was getting good money he could not bring himself to pay the small amount required. A second

[1] *Death in the Afternoon.*

and third notice came and finally his mother's remains were transferred to the public dump.

> 'What kind of blood is it in a man that will let that be done to his mother? You don't deserve to have a mother'.
> 'It is my mother', he said. 'Now she is so much dearer to me. Now I don't have to think of her buried in one place and be sad. Now she is all about me in the air, like the birds and the flowers. Now she will always be with me'.
> 'Jesus Christ', I said, 'what kind of blood have you any way? I don't want you even to speak to me'.[1]

The feeling expressed here is entirely traditional. At the time there was a growing movement in favour of regarding family ties as retrogressive and in addition materialism held corpses in little esteem.

In his last novel, *Across the River*, Hemingway seems to be under some compulsion to demonstrate his art-culture, or at least the Colonel's. As I have said, the Colonel is a whole person, fully credible though (to me) distasteful. I feel that he is a man who, having moved about a lot, has realised that the ability to talk on aesthetic matters carries with it a certain *éclat*. Knowledge of the arts is useful if for no other purpose than to impress. But there is also the possibility than Hemingway himself has (to use a metaphor he would understand) dropped his guard and let the cries of anticulture land on his body. Having done the work he was fitted for perhaps he wishes to show that he too can write intelligently about art. Rather late in his career he told

[1] 'The Mother of a Queen', from *Winner Take Nothing*.

Lillian Ross that he learned to write by looking at pictures. He has the painter's faculty of selection. Now he wishes to prove to us he has the critic's faculty of discrimination. I must admit, however, that if Huxley had not delivered his attack there might not be the temptation to reason in this way.

Early in the book the Colonel tells his driver he knows quite a little about painters. He shows his acquaintance with the work of Giotto and suggests acquaintance with that of Piera della Francesca and Mantegna and Michelangelo. He speaks with an air of great hidden knowledge, as though he could say a lot more if he wished. But he sounds tired and gives no sense of pleasure in what he knows. Against this is the fact that he *is* tired – but tired of life and war, whereas a man should not become tired of art, which is one way of making life supportable. He throws in odd references which add up to an insistence on a culture which is always below the surface. The great Canal 'was now becoming as grey as though Degas had painted it on one of his greyest days'. At times it becomes so forced as to be exasperating. When Renata's voice reminded him of Pablo Casals playing the cello I feel I have to state my conviction that this broken-down military tortoise cares no more about Casals than he does about Sunday School. I know – it's unfair, it's not criticism, it's a shocking indulgence in emotionalism. And Hemingway has his excellent defence that that is exactly what the Colonel did feel. He made him and knows; I didn't and don't. Well that's how I feel about the Colonel. But mark this: critics treated Jake Barnes as a typical representative of his generation. If we are to regard the Colonel as a typical representative of the same generation grown older, the degeneration is alarming.

When it's the literary art that he is discussing, Hemingway's touch is sure. There is no sense of strain. He is obviously a man who knows far more than he ever tells us. It is impossible to feel gaps in knowledge which he says no writer can hide. Even in a book on Big Game hunting the literary talk holds our attention. In fact, he tells us far more about the condition of American writing than he does about the animals, and in far fewer words. When his wife sees 'André's pictures' and Masson in the landscape, the note is again a trifle self-conscious. But the literary shop is good. Is there any reason why the writing profession should be the only one that should be forbidden to talk shop?

CHAPTER XI

FEELING AND SENSIBILITY

I HAVE finished discussing the major aspects of Hemingway's work and now intend to look more closely into some of the other elements which may have been taken for granted. For instance, in discussing his sense of tradition, his sense of frustration and the importance of fear I have not yet answered the central question: What is the extent of his sensibility? I think it is obvious that a writer of his calibre and achievement must possess a good store of sensibility yet so great is the emphasis on his hardness and lack of emotion there does seem to be a paradox here. The question really is: How does his sensibility gain its effect?

There is an astonishing touch of critical appreciation in *To Have and Have Not* which, for me at least, suddenly arrests the whole story. Like the image of a good poet, it is rare and its impact certain. (The rareness of his imagery is something which ought to have been noticed before – one only notices it consciously after reading some of the younger poets who believe that imagery *is* poetry and therefore the more imagery the more poetry.) At the most dangerous moment in Morgan's life, when he is taking a group of desperate Cuban revolutionaries back to their own country, he looks out 'across the grey swell of the Gulf Stream where the round red sun was just touching the water. 'Watch that. When she goes all the way under it'll turn bright green''.'

The Cuban is not impressed. 'The hell with that. You think you got away with something,' he says, and Harry hastily offers to get him another gun. But he has foreseen his own death in the setting sun, and he may even wonder what colour he'll turn.

Hemingway tells us why he is sparing in the use of 'sensibility', using the word in its popular sense. It is never easy to know what is true emotion, nor what produces it. He did not think he would like bullfights because he disliked seeing animals mal-treated. In other words, he was expending emotion on something he didn't know. He knew what it was to see mules have their legs broken and pushed into a harbour, and he didn't like it. His sensibility, his capacity to enter into the feelings of other creatures, was hurt and the resultant emotion was one of dis-tress, perhaps pity. Later he learnt that mules in Smyrna were by no means identifiable with bulls in Pamplona. Environment and purpose modify any impact on the sensibility and if these are unknown to you you cannot forecast your emotion accurately.

> I was trying to write then and I found the greatest difficulty, aside from knowing truly what you really felt, rather then what you were supposed to feel, and had been taught to feel, was to put down what really happened in action; what the actual things were which produced the emotion that you experienced.[1]

To get an emotion clean you must cast out the emotions which normally precede it. True objectiv-ity is a cleaning of the emotional slate so that you register a fresh response and without ambiguity.

[1] *Death in the Afternoon.*

Hunting in Africa assisted his search for the right frame of mind in which to approach the object and, incidentally, the right frame of mind improves the hunting. If you are after rhino it is best not to pity the animal in advance. Your object is to kill him and if you start admiring his vitality or his size or other qualities apart from his anatomical structure in relation to a bullet, your skill as a killer will be lessened. There are other times when you watch him for his other qualities. You must be quite clear about what you are doing. So he watched the rhino, 'freezing myself deliberately inside, stopping the excitement as you close a valve, going into that impersonal state you shoot from'.[1]

Edgar Johnson notices how, 'even more than Jake, Henry is immuring himself in an ivory tower of trying not to feel'.[2] This has nothing to do with art. It was an essential part of war. To leave your emotions bare was to court madness. It was the necessity of shutting out feeling that Hemingway, like Henry, learnt in war and later turned to artistic use. It was a valuable lesson. (Tolstoy had learnt it as the result of a similar experience: Ford Madox Ford kept the same tight hold of himself; it is one of the roots of the classical approach to phenomena, bred out of the proximity of suffering and danger.) When at last the nerves are overtaxed, or when the sensibility is intentionally bared under the delusion that the more naked it is the more it will assimilate, you

[1] *Green Hills of Africa.*
[2] 'Farewell the Separate Peace', from *Ernest Hemingway: the Man and his Work*, ed. J. McCaffery.

get the flood of uncontrolled emotion that can lead to madness. Kashkin in *For Whom the Bell Tolls* had apparently been such a case. And Philip in *The Fifth Column* admits that counter-espionage is 'getting on his nerves' and he fears his efficiency is suffering. Each profession must learn to close a part of its sensitivity. A writer must decide on the effect he is looking for and make all others impossible. It is this that Hemingway does so admirably.

So far we have discussed two central lessons in the art of expressing a true emotion: freezing all the pre-existent ones and only letting yourself go on what you actually see and feel. It was participation in war that taught these initial lessons. Hemingway draws attention to the fact that the pain of a wound does not start until about half an hour after it is sustained. If you do not know this and, in an effort of sensitive identification you begin to feel emotional distress immediately, you are wasting emotion and actually suffering worse agonies than the subject of the wound. Knowledge is as necessary in this field of artistic re-creation as in others.

> The pain of an abdominal wound does not come at the time but later with the gas pains and the beginnings of peritonitis; a pulled ligament or a broken bone, though, hurts at once and terribly; but these things are not known or they are ignored by the person who has identified himself with the animal and he will suffer genuinely and terribly, seeing only this aspect of the bullfight, while, when a horse pulls up lame in a steeplechase, he will not suffer at all and consider it merely regrettable.[1]

[1] *Death in the Afternoon.*

195

Some people read into this kind of objectivity a lack of feeling that makes it repugnant, even if it is true. It is a moralistic attitude, resulting from the belief that we ought to suffer in communion with other creatures, without any consideration of the quality. But Hemingway is thinking entirely of his craft as a writer, and the moral aspect must not be entertained during the search for accuracy. He does not scorn the vicarious sufferer, as is obvious from the last quotation, and in one place one of his characters even asserts the need for 'kindness', which is a product of sympathy. The revolutionary Max, in *The Fifth Column*, stresses the importance of this – incidentally negating Philip's dismissal of an allied humanist virtue, courtesy (already referred to). 'But remember to be kind,' says Max. 'To us to whom dreadful things have been done, kindness in all *possible* things is of great importance.' That is, in our relations with other people, even in war. But writing is concerned with relations to events and states of being – with people too, but only as components of events and states of being. They are being observed, not propitiated.

Those who see only Hemingway's hardness see too quickly and superficially. But the emotion is left to the reader. It is an interesting matter of literary fact that when the writer emphasises the emotion which he believes should be felt (Dickens' great fault) the reader becomes impatient. He is looking for his own emotions, he does not want to borrow them. Hemingway is on the right track. He presents a scene or an action and the reader completes it emo-

tionally. Henry Seidel Canby says that what impresses
him in Hemingway's work is not the hard-boiled
quality but the 'feeling for pathos without sentimentality' as in the study of Manuel in 'The Undefeated'
and the death in the hospital in *Farewell to Arms*
(Introduction to Modern Library Edition of *The Sun
Also Rises*).

It should be obvious by now that Hemingway
takes great care in the presentation of emotion. I
he leaves its experience to the reader he also has to
show how and when it is felt by the people in his
books. Again it is not always what we might expect.
For instance, Richard Gordon in *To Have and Have
Not* witnesses a horrible beating-up in a waterfront
bar ('When I hit him just then I felt his jaw go like
a bag of marbles'), and remains unmoved. What
really upsets Gordon is to hear about the old men in
New York who will let you piss in their beards for a
dollar. That makes him feel sick. Traditionally it is
the brutality of unprovoked assault that is sickening;
the other is merely disgusting. Trying to be dis-
passionate, one would be tempted to call both the
old men and the sailors perverts and leave it at that.
Yet it is frequently the minor things that upset the
emotional system more than the major ones which
are felt to challenge the security of our civilisation.
It is impossible to be categorical in these matters, but
it does illustrate Hemingway's method, based on the
closest observation.

The plain fact is that brutality is enjoyable.
Visit an all-in wrestling match if you want evidence.
Forget that the match was probably fixed and just

listen to the calls and comments of the crowd. You even get it at a football match where the opportunity is limited. I have already drawn attention to Hemingway's conviction that men enjoy killing. Fishing in Big Two-Hearted River is made more enjoyable by its brutality, even if this is usually evaded by the astonishing assertion that cold-blooded creatures feel no pain. It is also a wonderful joke to build a barricade and pot the enemy as they come over it. If it weren't so enjoyable people would cease to do it. There is no other way to account for the persistence of war, the defence of trade routes notwithstanding.

But there is a gentler side to Hemingway, a sphere in which the more agreeable forms of sensibility have their play. His appreciation of atmosphere is not confined to moments of violence and death. The difference between him and most other writers is the economy of his method. In comparison Osbert Sitwell, for instance, seems to be hopelessly entangled in a maze of words, many of which probably contribute nothing to the effect he seeks. He would take two pages at least to describe the difference between night and day. Hemingway merely says, 'It is awfully easy to be hard-boiled about everything in the daytime, but at night it is another thing,'[1] and it is enough. Later in the same book: 'There is no reason why because it is dark you should look at things differently from when it is light. The hell there isn't!' (This may be the only exclamation mark in Hemingway; it should be treasured.)

He is rather more loquacious when trying to establish feeling about place, but not very loquacious and in his somewhat awkward, colloquial terms he tells us exactly what he wants us to know.

> The Boulevard Raspail always made dull riding. It was like a certain stretch on the P.L.M. between Fontainebleau and Montereau that always made me feel bored and dull until it was over. I suppose it is some association of ideas that makes those dead places in a journey. There are other streets in Paris as ugly as the Boulevard Raspail. It is a street I do not mind walking down at all. But I cannot stand to ride along it.[1]

This is a subtle difference to notice and may be familiar to other people. It takes a sensitive writer to put it down. Many people can feel this but they usually describe their feelings by gestures, grimaces and silences.

Here is another piece of exact writing that appears much easier than it is. 'It was like certain dinners I remember during the war. There was much wine, an ignored tension, and a feeling of things coming that you could not prevent happening. Under the wine I lost the disgusted feeling and was happy. It seemed they were all such nice people.'[2] 'Ignored tension' is the phrase that works like magic.

These examples should reverse the popular belief that Hemingway's perception is limited to eye and hand. This is voiced by Lincoln Kirstein thus: 'he can only describe what he has seen with his eyes, touched with his hands. Not only does he mistrust any other perception, he virtually denies its possibil-

[1] *Fiesta.*
[2] *Ibid.*

ity'.[1] This is another instance of literary absolutism. The truth is that physical perception has primacy with Hemingway, but it is not solitary. That other sense which we call the sixth because we don't understand it (is there a parallel with the Third Programme?) is present in his work. It is especially strong in *Fiesta* and seems to have decayed with time.

Undoubtedly sense perception and feeling about place are closely bound up. The latter may be based on unspecific and unconscious memories which become transmuted into a sensation which cannot be localised or defined in analytic terms. For instance, the following wonderfully sharp passage from *For Whom the Bell Tolls* may be associated with and later productive of states of mind which will be more like an inhaled atmosphere than the reflection of physical perception:

> Pilar and the smell of death. This is the smell I love. This and fresh-cut clover, the crushed sage as you ride after cattle, wood-smoke and the burning leaves of autumn. That must be the odour of nostalgia, the smell of the smoke from the pile of raked leaves burning in the streets in the fall in Missoula. Which would you rather smell? Sweet grass the Indians used in their baskets? Smoked leather? The odour of the ground in the spring after rain? The smell of the sea as you walk through the gorse on a headland in Galicia? Or the wind from the land as you come in toward Cuba in the dark?

(In view of all these smells, and others I have not listed, it is interesting to note that Hemingway claims

[1] 'The Canon of Death', *Ernest Hemingway: the Man and his Work*, ed. McCaffery.

he does not smoke because it would affect his sense of smell – if not a rationalisation of distaste, another instance of his seriousness.) But it is possible that, after a period of gestation, any of these smells would give him a sense of death and decay because he has come to bracket them with what he calls 'the smell of death'. Some of them, the burning leaves and the crushed sage, are themselves images of decay and destruction yet others are equally images of life. But it must not be forgotten how important death is in Hemingway's feelings about life, how automatically life presents itself to him as a brief interlude in aeons of death. Remembering this, the link is clear.

Clarity of vision is the keynote. Just as the smells are sharply smelt, so the sights are sharply seen. In fact, a wound is to Hemingway an abstraction. Most of us regard woundedness as the abstraction, a wound as the physical reality. But Hemingway requires to visualise the wound. After all, a head wound is very different from a gut wound. A wound is only an intermediate stage, speaking semantically, between woundedness and the fact seen or felt. The real physical truth, on which the others depend, is a particular disposition of blood, bone and sinew. He describes how he saw a bullfighter gored in the thigh and how he woke up in the night trying to remember exactly what he had seen and what was its significance. Finally he got it.

> When he stood up, his face white and dirty and the silk of his breeches opened from waist to knee, it was the dirtiness of the rented breeches, the dirtiness of his slit underwear and the clean, clean, unbearably

clean whiteness of the thigh bone that I had seen, and it was that which was important.[1]

There is something of the miniaturist in Hemingway. Or perhaps that is wrong. A miniaturist reduces his scale, which Hemingway does not. He simply tries to find the unit of experience. It is a kind of literary atomisation, not over the whole working field but in carefully selected areas where the effect will be greatest. Hemingway once told Fitzgerald that the true death of a writer comes when he stops seeing – not when he stops feeling, for all feeling depends on the physical perception. Ideas float in the air. At the time when Hemingway made his reputation and when he had probably never opened a book of formal philosophy, one of the major concerns of philosophers was the determination of what really constituted perception. Hemingway's work in fiction ran parallel to these studies.

At the end of each section I always seem to return to Hemingway's acute insight into all matters concerning his own craft. Having created some of the best literature of our time he proceeds to deliver a few shrewd hints concerning its production. He has the keen and commonsense mind of Somerset Maugham in this respect. This may appear to have nothing to do with perception but it has a lot to do with sensibility, and as I have tried to show, the one always provides a base for the other in his work.

> All our early classics ... did not know that a new classic does not bear any resemblance to the classics

[1] *Death in the Afternoon.*

that have preceded it. It can steal from anything that it is better than, anything that is not a classic, all classics do that. Some writers are only born to help another writer to write one sentence. But it cannot derive from or resemble a previous classic.[1]

There is a direct line of communication between the writer who will use a whole body of work to perfect a single sentence and the writer who will reduce an event to its most naked terms. Hemingway begins with the alphabet and produces literature. There are others who begin with literature and spawn millions of meaningless letters. This helps to explain his constant frivolity when brought face to face with the acknowledged classics — the books he will recognise as good or great or magnificent and which he will perhaps enjoy as a reader but which are not of value to him as a writer in his particular field. 'Well, I guess some of us write and some of us pitch, but so far there isn't any law a man has to go and see *The Cocktail Party* by T. S. Eliot from St. Louis, where Yogi Berra comes from.'[2] There are some who would regard this as vaguely shocking; they are the hangers-on of literature who require a First Class Honours Degree in English Literature before they attempt their own masterpieces. I doubt if Eliot would regard it as shocking.

[1] *Green Hills of Africa*.
[2] 'Talk With Mr. Hemingway', Harvey Breit, *New York Times*, 17 Sept. 1950.

CHAPTER XII

A GLIMPSE OF BEAUTY

A T the centre of the Western aesthetic tradition is the concept of beauty. Keats' identification of truth with beauty was largely accepted by the poets and artists who followed him, was reinforced by the Impressionists, Imagists and Cubists and only began to be attacked as a sound hypothesis after the onslaught of Dada and the Proletarians. Hemingway is not an aesthetic philosopher but there are ideas inherent in his work. I have chosen his view of Beauty in an attempt to contrast his attitude with the traditional one.

To begin with, he decapitalises beauty. Just as he cannot abstract the idea of a wound, so to him beauty is always concrete, always a representative and living fact. Somewhere behind his conception of beauty lies an affirmation of the Keatsian view, but it is presented in actual, perceptible terms. The best instance I can give comes from the story 'The Light of the World'[1] which is one of his favourites but which, rather significantly, he says no one else ever liked. Alice, 'the biggest whore I ever saw in my life and the biggest woman', had, a beauty which shone through her grossness. The difference between Alice and the other whores, apart from size, was that there was a simple truth in her. When the others boasted you could tell they were lying. But Alice had one proud memory, of the time when a fighter much

[1] From *Winner Take Nothing*.

coveted by women had had her and told her she was
a lovely piece, but that was a long time ago and it
was true. 'Alice looked at her and then at us and her
face lost that hurt look and she smiled and she had
about the prettiest face I ever saw. She had a pretty
face and a nice smooth skin and a lovely voice and
she was nice all right and really friendly. But my God
she was big.'

I think it was this treatment of Alice that made
the normal Hemingway fan feel uncomfortable. It
was a lapse from the hard-boiled. At the time it appeared people did not want to find a mingled truth
and beauty shining from a broken-down old whore.
They wanted to see her as something vicious because
everything was to be treated as the symbol or product
of a rotten society.

Hemingway's normal method of describing an
emotion (in this case, felt beauty) is to describe the
physical reaction of the beholder. It has something
in common with Vernon Lee's method but is not so
silly. Describing a horse he says, 'I never saw such a
horse. He was being led around the paddocks with
his head down and when he went by me I felt all
hollow inside he was so beautiful.'[1]

This is brief but genuine and recognisable. What
is not so satisfactory is his more familiar method of
surrendering to the difficulty of description and falling back on the cliché of the business man. For
instance, 'Brett was damned good-looking'. But in
many cases he switches immediately to the responsibility of the writer, as here: 'She wore a slip-over

[1] 'My Old Man', from *In Our Time*.

jersey sweater and a tweed skirt, and her hair was brushed back like a boy's. She started all that. She was built with curves like the hull of a racing yacht, and you missed none of it with that wool jersey.'[1] The picture of a writer and the emotion of a Rotarian.

This kind of approach suited the character of the Colonel in *Across the River* admirably. The Colonel is the Rotarian in uniform. As the novel is a projection of his own consciousness there is no need for the writer's contribution. (Hemingway is cunning: the writing is in the third person but all the thinking is the Colonel's.) He admired the lines of some fishing boats. 'It's not that they are picturesque. The hell with picturesque. They are just damned beautiful.' A little later he sees the expensive mistress of a Milanese profiteer and thinks, 'She is a beautiful, hard piece of work. She is damned beautiful, actually'.

This is 'a literature which has nothing to do with literature'. It has to do with the familiar world of inarticulateness and the sense of shame and irritation which the typical modern feels when faced by something beautiful. The rest is silence.

[1] *Fiesta.*

CHAPTER XIII

MORALITY: OR FEELING GOOD

SOMEWHERE behind this attitude of Hemingway's that I have diagnosed lies a morality. Again,
it will be convenient to start from the popular view
of the matter. Just as Faulkner is dubbed decadent,
so Hemingway is believed to project an entirely
immoral view of conduct.

There is an implicit code of conduct in the behaviour of most of Hemingway's characters. It derives
from admiration for and observance of the physical
virtues, courage and endurance. Lincoln Kirstein
says, quite truly, that moral courage has little place
in this code. 'He is not busied with the courage of the
mind, the energy of a moral activity restless in its
penetration to the heart of truth, unflinching at any
self-imposed limits.'[1] The code is based on those
things that people enjoy doing and therefore it is
very rarely indeed that anyone has to oppose his will
to his desires. Thus morality in the conventional sense
is scarcely recognised. The code consists of the minimum regulations for a life without responsibility; it
resembles the rules drawn up by a club for the regu-
lation of conduct.

The code is a sportsman's. It aims not at a high
quality in human relations but at sporting efficiency.
But whenever a group of people set out to determine
what constitutes efficiency they inevitably diverge

[1] These vile phrases come from 'The Canon of Death', in
Ernest Hemingway: the Man and his Work, ed. J. McCaffery.

from normal attitudes and start finding virtues in actions that are meaningless to others. For instance, it would be widely recognised that courage, honesty and skill are valuable in their pursuits, but only the initiates realise that clipped speech, the avoidance of emotion and the constant use of expletives are also essential elements. The code is best illustrated in *Fiesta,* particularly in the passages where Cohn persistently breaks it by refusing to admit defeat, by discussing his own emotions, and by being altogether too loquacious about certain 'banned' subjects. He is finally morally defeated by Romero, the matador, who refuses to surrender even when he has been repeatedly knocked down by Cohn. Another instance in the same novel is when Jake Barnes decides to get rid of Cohn by taking him to a café and then excusing himself because he has to send off some cables. He had work to do but could not admit it. 'It is very important to discover graceful exits like that in the newspaper business, where it is such an important part of the ethics that you should never seem to be working.'

Sometimes we see two codes making contact, but rarely with happy results. Jake Barnes was made to feel very uncomfortable during the fiesta as a result of one such contact. He himself could enter with assurance into the circle of bullfighters and aficionados but it was a different world from that of Paris and he knew it. One great difference, for instance, was that in bullfighting circles work was the first thing, not something that you pretended did not exist. A bullfighter was a serious workman. His attitude to drink and sex was therefore the reverse of an expatriate newspaper man's. In the one code work made drink and sex possible; in the other work could suffer from them. When Jake's companion, Lady Brett Ashley, seduced Romero it was equivalent to expulsion from a club for Jake, who had introduced them to each other. Women are a normal part of a bullfighter's life but Romero was young and very promising and the fiesta was not yet finished. Montoya, Jake's host at the hotel and an enthusiastic supporter of the bullring, ceased to speak to him. Jake could not allow his unhappiness to show itself, there was no one he could confide in, but his silence and acceptance are painful to the reader.

The real difference between this code and the others with which we are familiar, including the sportsman's, is that it has no reason for existence. 'There is no reason for obeying the code, no sense that somehow it sustains a society and a way of life.'[1] It is at first sight the most artificial code that has ever been invented. We must grant that it has an object, even if the object appears to be outside the sphere of either morality or immorality, but there is no relevance between code and object. To enjoy yourself on the physical plane there is no compulsion to deflate language and smother emotion. In fact, many Elizabethans did just the opposite in pursuit of similar ends.

Schwartz goes on to say that despite his alleged

[1] Delmore Schwartz, 'Ernest Hemingway's Literary Situation', from *Ernest Hemingway: the Man and his Work*, ed. J. McCaffery.

contempt for the 'glory' words and attitudes (which I have quoted in an earlier chapter) it is just these ideals that do in fact constitute the values contained in Hemingway's writing. There is a lot of truth in this. Is there any real difference between the man who wishes to win glory in war and the man who bases his conduct on admiration for courage? The first will realise his aim by acts of courage, the second is acknowledging one of the military virtues. The real change is in vocabulary. Literature oscillates between classicism and romanticism, baroque and rococo, sentiment and reason, and is paralleled by similar movements in the colloquial use of language. Rhetoric is forbidden, yet there is a need for it. Therefore Hemingway searches for a character who uses rhetoric unconsciously and therefore unrhetorically to express desires somewhat outside of common experience. Briefly, '*the foreigner* is necessary for this rhetoric'.[1] He takes his native idiom into English and the difference in tone emphasises the quality that cannot be similarly emphasised by the born Englishman or American. Or if the honourable one is an American he speaks in a special kind of American, not inflated, of course, but slightly off the normal key. This device is used throughout *For Whom the Bell Tolls*, and gives it the heroic flavour.

One writer has referred to 'the sturdy moral backbone' in *Fiesta*.[2] This is nonsense, resulting from the urge towards simplification. Having been attacked

[1] Schwartz, *ibid*.
[2] Carlos Baker, 'Twenty-Five Years of a Hemingway Classic', *New York Times Book Review*, 29 April 1951.

as an immoralist, Hemingway is now to be praised as a pillar of society. Mr. Baker contrasts the healthy boyishness of the Burguete episode with the vanities of the Montparnassian section. This is to suppose that a man who enjoys drinking and 'sleeping around', in the modern American phrase, cannot possibly enjoy fishing. It is equivalent to the mistake made by older people who, seeing young men enjoying themselves, claim that they have lost all moral fibre and will surrender to the first difficulty. Contrasting Burguete and Montparnasse throws no light on moral attitudes. A sensible person will get what he can out of experience and he will indulge in the experience that is best fitted to the environment. I mean, he will not seek a legshow in church or try high-diving in the desert. The joy of life to the ordinary man whose morals are not always agitating him consists in being very naughty one moment and very good (healthy, of course) the next.

Morality exists on different levels of intensity and subtlety. On the ordinary level of honesty, decent behaviour towards other people and not deceiving your friends, Hemingway acquits himself satisfactorily. John Peale Bishop said he could not be bought and referred to an occasion when Hemingway, living in considerable poverty at the time, turned down an attractive Hearst offer.

Now this is very interesting. Undoubtedly that was a moral action – Hemingway wished to remain in charge of his soul. It is the kind of thing that is applauded in writers and artists yet we know quite well that it rarely happens and no one really expects it to happen. But Hemingway's sense of morality is in direct contrast to the dominant Puritan one; it is judged by its effects, but moral conduct should bring with it a feeling of fulfilment, not of self-righteousness. The Puritan code tends to stress unpleasantness until we reach the point where an action is performed merely because it is unpleasant or difficult. Nothing could be further from Hemingway's practice. (It is true that he will attempt the difficult but simply out of his competitiveness, not out of any righteous glow.) The aim in life should be enjoyment and the truly moral life will be the one in which enjoyment is attained. The necessary corollary is that you should not hurt other people, i.e. attain to enjoyment at the expense of others.

> So far, about morals, I know only that what is moral is what you feel good after and what is immoral is what you feel bad after and judged by these moral standards, which I do not defend, the bullfight is very moral to me because I feel very fine while it is going on and have a feeling of life and death and mortality and immortality, and after it is over I feel very sad but very fine.[1]

This is empirical and workaday and not deeply thought, nor is it attached to any principle save a personal one, but it is only an intellectual convention that we should deduce moral principles from rational criteria. Hemingway probably felt sad but fine after rejecting the Hearst offer.

The best illustration of the Hemingway ethic appears in *Fiesta*. Jake liked to see Mike Campbell

[1] *Death in the Afternoon.*

hurt Cohn's feelings. (It made him feel good.) But afterwards he felt disgusted. (You should not hurt other people.) 'That was morality; things that made you disgusted afterwards. No, that must be immorality.'

He has a very modern sense of relativity in all these matters which are not susceptible to exact measurement. For instance, the term decadence has no real meaning when used without context. One person's decadence is another's health. 'Decadence is a difficult word to use since it has become little more than a term of abuse applied by critics to anything they do not yet understand or which seems to differ from their moral concepts'[1] He illustrates this with a story of Jean Cocteau's complaint about Radiguet: '*Bébé est vicieuse – il aime les femmes.*' When attitudes are so widely separated only a personal morality is possible. But conflicting personal moralities will lead either to perpetual warfare or the victory of one over all the others – as has happened, officially at least. But Hemingway does not consider this point. He is not really concerned with morality but with his own psychological wellbeing.

He does return frequently, however, to the attack on an imposed code of morality which relieves people of the task of thought. For instance, a universal code eventually leads to hypocrisy, again through the instrumentality of ignorance, which in turn is based on mental laziness. The English-born ex-Queen of Spain insisted that the picador's horse should be protected by a *peto* or mattress, covering the animal's chest, right flank and belly. This satisfied the humanitarians who ignored the rather ghastly consequences. Having charged the mattress without satisfactory result, the bulls tend to draw back. The picador then feels compelled to turn the unprotected hindquarters of his mount towards the bull. The result is that the horse, instead of being killed as in the old days, is constantly gored in the rear, patched up and brought back for other bulls.

> The frank admission of the necessity for killing horses to have a bullfight has been replaced by a hypocritical semblance of protection which causes the horses much more suffering but, once implanted, will be maintained as long as possible, because it saves the horse-contractor money, enabling the promoters to save money and allowing the authorities to feel that they have civilised the bullfight.[1]

The only hope for morality is to do away with it and it lies with the scientists to abolish diseases to that end. Morality thrives on immorality and as one cannot exist without the other and both are meaningless in isolation it is necessary to find physical facts that will act as symbols. The familiar ones are health and disease and it would be much better to abolish the latter than to make rules for its avoidance. In this happy-go-lucky type of reasoning which Hemingway conducts with such a large piece of his tongue in his cheek he would probably rank hypocrisy and unnecessary ignorance along with gonorrhea, which at least in one instance improved a champion golfer's putting.

[1] *Death in the Afternoon.*

With the Left-wing phase and the newly
acquired conception of social responsibility Hemingway's characters become more conventional in their
view of what ought and ought not to be done. There
is, at most, very little moralism in Hemingway's work
and of what there is most is to be found in *The Fifth
Column*. Philip, who appears to be one of the old
Lost Generation trying to reform himself, is fair
game for Dorothy. 'Philip, you must promise me
something. You won't just go on drinking and not
have any aim in life and not do anything real? You
aren't just going to be a Madrid playboy, are you?'
She sounds as though she might be Philip's conscience
but in fact the voice of conscience is still the old
voice of hypocrisy, working on a new terrain. It is
Philip, with all his weaknesses and inconsistencies,
who is the more truly moral of the two, simply because he is honest and does not lie either to himself
or to others. While Dorothy is identifying herself
with the people's cause she is buying fur capes in
shell-racked Madrid.

> DOROTHY: But, *darling*. It's so cheap. The foxes only
> cost twelve hundred pesetas apiece.
> PHILIP: That's one hundred and twenty days' pay
> for a man in the brigades. Let's see. That's four
> months. I don't believe I know anyone who's been
> out four months without being hit – or killed.

Philip reproaches her in a cold fury. He can see
that such spending is hurting people and that is forbidden by his code. He himself cannot utter moralist
sentiments, he knows how easily they lay one open to

reprisals and the charge of hypocrisy. It is contrasted not only with the falsity of Dorothy but also with the genuineness of Max, the revolutionary, who knows quite well why they are fighting: 'You do it so *every one* will have a good breakfast like that. You do it so *no one* will ever be hungry. You do it so men will not have to fear ill-health or old age; so they can live and work in dignity and not as slaves.'

In Philip, even more clearly than in Robert Jordan, we see the lack of a firm base for conduct. I suspect that Jordan is only a development of Richard Gordon, the writer, in *To Have and Have Not*. The similarity of the names suggested it, and we know that Jordan had an intellectual background which most of Hemingway's characters have not. Gordon had been an ineffective social realist and it is possible that he plunged into the Spanish War to protect his conscience. Philip is in the line of Jake Barnes and even his creator – he refers scornfully to the irresponsible life of the metropolitan hotels and flying out to Nairobi, but he speaks as one who has done it. He is conscious of his past, of his personal morality, and now he is expiating it through the discomforts of war, but war on the right side. He has lost the right to lay down any moral law because he cannot throw off his past completely. A man of imagination can no longer 'feel good' in such a situation. As Hemingway had said earlier, the only thing to do was to get on with your job and leave the programmes to others.

CHAPTER XIV

LOVE AND SEX

Sʜɪꜰᴛꜱ in emphasis, as illustrated by the usage
of words and ideas, are landmarks in human development. One of the most interesting and important of
these in modern times is the popular assumption that
morality means sexual morality. This is not the place
to discuss this limitation in the field of morality but
it has had a considerable effect on the public's appreciation of Hemingway and other writers who have
written frankly of sexual matters. It is probable that
this view has been partly formed by the writers themselves, though in many cases due to faulty understanding.

Hemingway has referred in *Death in the Afternoon* to that most important phase in individual
development, the discovery of sex (not necessarily
synonymous with either puberty or even adolescence).
Whatever the society there is a moment when the
individual is conscious for the first time of his sexual
power. The effect of this discovery will vary according to the earlier background and training, the existence of tabus and the degree of social inhibition, but
it is always important. Hemingway, in the passage
referred to, is concerned with 'college-boys', i.e. boys
from the more privileged section of society, more
than normally intelligent, and from 'good' homes.

A few years ago I had the opportunity of observing the
rakes' progress of some citizens who, in college, were
great moral influences, but after coming out into the

world discovered the joys of immorality, which, as believers in Yale in China, they had never indulged in as young men, and, delivering themselves to these joys, seemed to believe that they had discovered, if not indeed invented, sexual intercourse. They believed that this was the great new thing that they had just, discovered and were most joyously promiscuous until their first experience with disease which they then believed they too had discovered and invented.

The realisation of this hitherto unknown power is temporarily a source of great animal joy. This is a matter of sex only, which Hemingway is reputed to identify with love – or rather, which has replaced love in his work. The joy, in any intensity at least, is short-lived. Before realisation it has had to overcome several obstacles, chief of which are religious belief, timidity and fear of disease. The latter remains with many men as an obstacle to promiscuity. But with the man of action, Hemingway's special concern, this fear is pushed into the background. Illustrating from the life of a bullfighter (probably more typical of the man of action than we may at first sight suppose) Hemingway says that promiscuity is practically obligatory: it is part of the tradition, women seek him for various reasons – and, constantly exposed to danger in his work, the bullfighter scorns venereal disease as a minor and rarely lethal danger.

I have prefaced my discussion of Hemingway's treatment of sex and love in this way because it is with the man of action that we are chiefly concerned. We will not find it necessary, for instance, to examine the sexual morality of college professors or reflective men in general though we shall meet a college teacher

who has adopted the life of action. All these men
have overcome early qualms and fears about sex and
none of them, so far as we can gather, allow the possibility of disease to dilute their pleasure. They have
also passed beyond the springtime joy of discovery
and regard sex as a natural appetite whose satisfaction is pleasurable.

It is the college teacher turned man of action,
Robert Jordan, who dispels the charge that Hemingway's characters do not distinguish between love and
sex. He is the right man for the job. Apart from the
Colonel, he is the only one who searches himself for
motives or attempts to understand his own feelings.
He draws a very sharp distinction between sleeping
with a 'casual piece' (which is pleasant but no more
than 'just dragging ashes') and the emotion of love.
'When I am with Maria I love her so that I feel, literally, as though I would die and I never believed in
that nor thought that it could happen.' My impression
is that both Frederick Henry and Jake Barnes felt the
same, although they never allowed it to become conscious, and that, like Jordan, they came to learn that
there is another quality that transmutes sex into love.
Both were frustrated – the tragedy of Jake's life was
that he probably never understood what love might
be until it was too late. He is a man who wants
desperately to love but knows that its consummation
is not possible.

We must not confuse the distinction between
love and sex with their division. There is a sense, a
mystical sense, in which love can exist without the
other. We do not find this in Hemingway, where

everyone is fully aware of his animal nature. The possibilities are sex without love or love based on sex, and it is the latter that Jordan affirms. He does not do it easily. Although the socially accepted view of love today is that it requires the sexual experience for its fulfilment, Jordan came from an intellectual milieu that doubted this and was only too prone to regard the love element as a species of sentimentalism which disguised a rather sordid fact. He went through an inward struggle in which his old convictions fought hard to belittle the new emotion. He knew that Pilar had laid the trap, that she had 'pushed the girl into your sleeping bag'. So it was the same old story, then, lust, only by some biological accident more satisfying than usual in its result. But there was this new feeling that he couldn't deny and at last he had to admit it – he had slept with many women but he had never felt like this about any of them. 'It hit you then and you know it so why lie about it? You went all strange inside every time you looked at her and every time she looked at you.'

Hemingway is as aware as any writer of the immediate and annihilating attack of emotion that accompanies a sexual relationship, especially among the young, but he also knows that all traces of it can disappear just as quickly. When Nick learns that his Prudie has been seen with another man he waits till his father leaves the room and then cries. 'My heart's broken,' he thought. 'If I feel this way my heart must be broken.'[1] In bed he heard the wind in the trees and forgot to think about Prudence. 'In the morning

[1] 'Ten Indians', from *Men Without Women*.

there was a big wind blowing and the waves were
running high up on the beach and he was awake a
long time before he remembered that his heart was
broken.'

Hemingway is not the kind of writer who makes
'points' but I think the feeling behind this story
and other similar accounts is that this has nothing in
common with the powerful emotion that has appealed
to the romantic poets. It is largely a question of age.
When Robert Jordan is affected in the same way the
emotion is mature and lasting, or at least, not merely
temporary. The young feel the emotion, perhaps even
more strongly than they feel the physical desire, but
they are not yet ready for it. It passes through them,
they have not yet become strong enough to hold it.
First of all they must overcome their ignorance.
Knowing the facts of copulation has nothing to do
with it. The ignorance is emotional ignorance and it
is impossible even to consider what love really is
until the unfamiliarity is overcome. In 'Up In
Michigan' Liz is in a state of utter bewilderment.
She wants something desperately, she only knows
vaguely what it is, she is hurt, she wants Jim to love
her and she wants him not to do what he is doing,
she is frightened, and she feels a wonderful tenderness for him.[1]

Hemingway sees three stages in the sex-love
complex. First, there is the youthful stage of uncon-
trollable, un-understood feeling, which is nothing
more than initial exploration, however powerfully
it affects the individual. Then comes retreat into sex

[1] *In Our Time.*

only. The third stage, which does not come until the others have been fully experienced, is that of full understanding, truly-felt love realised through sex. In 'Soldier's Home',[1] which many people consider his finest story, the retired soldier Krebs has emerged from the second stage. He will either remain there or he will go forward into the third. He no longer needed a girl, as men are usually and crudely assumed to need a girl. Yet he sat watching the girls passing by and he liked looking at them.

> Vaguely he wanted a girl but he did not want to have to work to get her. He would have liked to have a girl but he did not want to spend a long time getting her. He did not want to get into the intrigue and the politics. He did not want to have to do any courting. He did not want to tell any more lies. It wasn't worth it.

This account of a stage in a man's attitude towards women is one of the truest things Hemingway has ever written. It represents the state of complete seriousness in which a man must approach love if he is to have it at all. The shams have all been sloughed off. There is no need to pretend that you are a great lover, that you have an unslakeable thirst, that you are a gay dog, that you are superior to others. Krebs discovered that French and German girls were really preferable to Americans because he could not talk to them. It was talking that spoilt the reality of love. Speech introduced complications outside the field of love. Having tongues people felt obliged to use them. If you did not spend the time showing off you were liable to create situations, just out of care-

[1] *Ibid.*

less words or even malicious but not seriously meant
words, that led to misunderstanding. You found yourself in that ridiculous situation when you were being
unkind to the one person for whom kindness alone
was intended. Frederick Henry once wished he could
cut off his tongue.

> 'Oh darling!' she came back from wherever she had
> been. 'You mustn't mind me'. We were both together
> again and the self-consciousness was gone. 'We really
> are the same one and we mustn't misunderstand on
> purpose'.
> 'We won't'.
> 'But people do. They love each other and they mis-
> understand on purpose and they fight and then
> suddenly they aren't the same one'.

This feeling of identity is a familiar and necessary
experience for lovers. It is something transcendental
and words, coming out of the world of time and
triviality, are its chief enemy. Henry and Catherine
are strongly aware of it, especially at night. A sour
critic might argue that this is because their relationship was, despite the lofty feelings they professed for
each other, only sexual. But that would not ring true.
The importance of the night was the close contact
without the necessity of words or the distraction of
vision, a complete physical and spiritual unity.

Theodore Bardacke, referring to the part played
by love and sex in *Fiesta*, says that Hemingway writes
of the lost relationship between love and sex. But
this is true only of that novel, where Jake knows love
without sex and Brett sex without love. I have
referred to the symbolic significance of Jake's impo-

tence and Bardacke interprets Harry Morgan's satisfying relationship with his wife as 'a measure of his affirmative strength and an adjustment to the world'.[1] I am also tempted to interpret a gruesome incident in one of the stories in the same way. An Alpine peasant's wife had died but he had not been able to bring her body for burial because of the snow. He kept it in his shed where it became frozen. When he worked there at nights he used to hang his lantern from her mouth. Perhaps this is a horrible story. As the innkeeper said, 'All these peasants are beasts'. Yet when the priest asked the peasant if he loved his wife he replied, 'Ja, I loved her. I loved her fine'.[2] There is a simplicity about the story and a dignity about the peasant which appeals far more to me than the usual passionate affirmations. The couple had lived a hard life together, sharing cold and hardship, and always helping each other. They probably did not speak much together. Their life together had been a partnership for the simple purpose of living their time with as little discomfort as they could manage. It did not occur to the peasant that he was outraging his wife's body putting it to such obvious use. (It was obvious to him when he looked round for a place to hang his lantern.) The partnership continued to the very day of final separation.

It is in the more sophisticated and thoughtful sectors of society that we find the rhetoric of love and also of its failure. The dying writer in 'The

[1] 'Hemingway's Women', from *Ernest Hemingway: the Man and his Work*, ed. J. McCaffery.
[2] 'An Alpine Idyll', from *Men Without Women*.

Snows of Kilimanjaro', who would never have put his wife's body to any useful purpose (not even child-bearing, one suspects), says, 'love is a dunghill. And I'm the cock that gets on it to crow'. Helen Gordon in *To Have and Have Not* exclaims that

> love is just another dirty lie. Love is ergoapiol pills to make me come around because you were afraid to have a baby. Love is quinine and quinine and quinine until I'm deaf with it. Love is that dirty aborting horror that you took me to. Love is my insides all messed up. It's half catheters and half whirling douches. I know about love. Love always hangs up behind the bath-room door. It smells like lysol. To hell with love.

All these words are a counter-attack against the beautiful words that had preceded them, the love-was-all-that-mattered words, what-we-have-and-no-one-else, you-little-back-flower. The writer is sniping against all his fellow-writers who he feels have misled him. We see these very articulate people, loving beautifully, passionately and romantically, contrasted with the Morgans who love in grunts and converse in monosyllables. And Richard Gordon snootily pities Mrs. Morgan who is obviously an animal and could never rise to love. And we know that the chief difference between these people is that the Gordons have learnt new ways in which to mess up love and the Morgans have found fulfilment without innovation.

The violence that we associate with Hemingway and which he finds in war, sport and the bullring is also part of his view of love. Except for the love affairs that he has spotlighted, the more successful ones such as Frederick Henry's and Catherine Barkley's, there is little tenderness. The feeling between Harry Morgan and his wife, though sincere, is more like that of a conflict than of a harmonious partnership. It would be truer to say that they find harmony in conflict. The lovers in the stories (I am using lover in its broadest sense) treat each other as obstacles to be overcome rather than personalities who must mutually give and take. The Gordons fight each other and even in the past, when they must have persuaded themselves that they were experiencing the more tender passages of love, the basic struggle that Hemingway finds in all living must have been close to the surface. Men and women must either reflect this conflict in their own relations or co-operate to lessen its consequences. Perhaps that is why the action of the Alpine peasant was so acceptable, despite the disgust it arouses. According to Malcolm Cowley, Hemingway 'falls in love like a big hemlock tree crashing down through the underbrush'.

That is a highly personal judgment and perhaps it should not be recorded in a work of literary criticism. Lest it give the wrong impression I will add that Hemingway abhors the kind of cocktail-flirtation that became so common in the twenties among the people of whom he wrote. But his conception of love is intensely romantic. Each individual becomes a whole world unto himself, and every minor setback tends to be regarded as a catastrophe of cosmic proportions. In this type of relationship, sanctified by the Victorians, aptly dubbed *égoisme à deux*, the individual is alone of significance. Frederick Henry and Catherine Barkley tried to build themselves an ivory tower in Switzerland. To crash like a hemlock tree is to pull down more than yourself, like Samson, to imagine for the moment of falling that you are greater than you are, that in your personal destiny is bound up a much wider destiny. But this, with many other like attitudes, faded during the Spanish War. Philip, in *The Fifth Column*, no longer regards the night as the time when the ultimate purposes of life are revealed. Love or sex, symbolised by the night, must be related to other activities. 'Never believe what I say in the night,' he says. 'I lie like hell in the night.'

There is a constant reference in his work to the night as an entity with special significance. To Frederick and Catherine it was the hour of revelation. Even for Robert Jordan, who has partially rejected the old individualist romanticism, the night still holds its immense power. It was in the night that his old flames came back to him, not so much in orthodox dreams as in a kind of wish-fulfilment, always much more satisfying than they had been in actuality. He had even had Garbo and Harlow in that way. But it was all part of an irresponsible past, before he had learnt that he was a person of no importance, or at most a particle in a commonwealth. But Philip had sorted these things out properly. In the light of day he knew exactly the relationship between his own personal love and that greater responsibility to all people. And so he tells Dorothy that he doesn't love her in the daytime.

The question is, in the midst of all these complications, whether a fully satisfying love is possible

in these times. The history of Frederick Henry illustrates the predicament. At first love is inadmissible.
He shares the young-lion attitude towards it of his
time, that, love is an outworn posture. John W.
Aldridge in *After the Lost Generation* suggests that
love is like death, its oblivion leads to the total extinction of the personality. I feel this is far-fetched. It
is simply a posture and, like all postures, easily
broken. In his hospital conversation with the priest,
Henry says he doesn't love but it is obvious that he
wants to. He is thinking of the nights he has spent
and how empty they were, and he is puzzled by the
new emotion Catherine has roused in him. It is not
easy to drop a pet theory, especially when you are
young and believe you have a powerful intuition for
these things, lost by the older generation. And even
when he discovers that love is real the discovery is
mocked by the event that wipes out the love he had.
So far as Henry's personal experience went love was
possible but circumstances always conspired against
it and after savouring it you lost it. So the question
remains: Is Love Possible? I asked Hemingway and
he answered, 'Every man knows that for himself. For
me it is'.

The curse that seems to lie on a fulfilled love
is an important element in his work. *Farewell to
Arms, To Have and Have Not* and *For Whom the
Bell Tolls* are all love stories where one of the lovers
dies prematurely and we care very much. Even in the
case of Harry Morgan, although we may feel the
world has lost little by his death, we know his wife
has lost much. There is the same situation in *Across*

the River, where an ageing lover dies of heart failure, as we might expect him to do, but it is hard to see how anyone could care. Yet there is Renata. Why on earth did Renata love the Colonel? Was it pity, a young evangelist's pity for a bitter, egotistical old bore? Before attempting an answer I would like to draw attention at this convenient point to one of the major weaknesses of modern criticism. It lies in arrogance, of which this field is full. Almost the universal answer to the question I have put would be that Renata couldn't love the Colonel, being what she was and he being what he was. (The critic often says 'I could not believe in X', as though that matters.) The reasons would be tabulated and expounded at length. But it would be argument out of ignorance. No critic has the right to quarrel with a character's behaviour, because human behaviour is infinitely variable. Phrases such as 'consistency of character' are question-begging and smell of the study. If Hemingway says these two were in love we must accept it for he alone knows. We are not to question the love although we have the right to seek its cause. It could be pity but that is no denial of love. Pity is one of the many bases of love.

It may be a rash thing to say but there is a possibility that Hemingway may be as intelligent, as sensitive, as intuitive, as inquiring, as truthful, as sincere as his critics. Whether this be true or not, the question did enter his mind: Why did Renata love the Colonel? He sets the Colonel to grapple with this problem which is really the underlying concern of the whole novel.

But how could she love a sad son of a bitch like you?
I do not know, he thought truly. I truly do not know.
He did not know, among other things, that the girl
loved him because he had never been sad one waking
morning of his life; attack or no attack. He had experienced anguish and sorrow. But he had never been sad
in the morning.
They make almost none like that and the girl, although she was a young girl, knew one when she saw
one.

All that it is possible to say to this is that it may
be true. Many a love must have been worn away by
morning sourness and the act of faith implicit in
morning cheerfulness may be the seed of much
beauty. But it is impossible to be categorical about
it. If we make literature a department of psychology
it will be the death of literature. We should only
demand vitality of utterance and the natural exuber-
ance of a man who is fully alive. As for this interpretation of Renata's love, I don't like it. It sounds too
much to me like the Great American Naif stamping
the prairies – but I am not naïf enough to deny its
possible truth.

This is a difficult love affair to come to terms
with because we have been conditioned by our
stupendous romantic legacy. An ageing soldier with
cardiac trouble and a beautiful young Italian count-
ess. We are so unfamiliar with the literary portrayal
of such a relationship we find it difficult to give it
full allegiance. The situation in *Farewell to Arms*
is entirely familiar and we warm to it even before
it has begun. As soon as we hear of Miss Barkley we
know it must begin. The love affair in *For Whom the*

Bell Tolls might have been a repetition but it wasn't. In the first novel all is simplicity and the indescribable elements of love are merely implied. In the later novel there is an attempt to describe the indescribable and the writing is often forced and strained. In this novel Hemingway attempts what has so far been impossible and still remains unachieved, a man's emotional state in the midst of intercourse.

> For him it was a dark passage which led to nowhere, then to nowhere, then again to nowhere, once again to nowhere, always and for ever to nowhere, heavy on the elbows in the earth to nowhere, dark, never any end to nowhere, this time and again for always to nowhere, now not to be borne once again always and to nowhere, now beyond all bearing up, up, up and into nowhere, suddenly, scaldingly, holdingly all nowhere gone and time absolutely still and they were both there, time having stopped and he felt the earth move out and away from under them.

It would be a monstrous thing to mock this bold attempt, armed with the full power of a fine writer, to storm one of life's strongpoints—yet I feel this is a point that cannot be taken and the enlistment of thaumaturgy in the service of explicitness must fail. The enfolding of the sexual act in the before and after, as in *Farewell to Arms*, is the nearest we can get.

There is absolutely no straining in *Farewell to Arms*. The continual repetition of 'do you love me?' is its chief strength. That the words are trite and, in a semantic sense, almost without meaning is beside the point. Only a full sympathy between writer and reader can establish their full value. The early cynicism dissolves in these monosyllables and their impact can best be clarified by a parallel with, say, the Horst Wessel song – a dull, uninspired melody to the outsider but a wonder-working one to the initiate. (I must apologise for this example but I needed one with the necessary contrast.)

But the predominating tone of Hemingway's treatment of the love theme is its temporary nature. There is no such thing as a lasting love. In Frederick Henry's case, where he is left mourning a statue, it might be objected that this is by no means a universal experience. We must not generalise from the accidental. But Catherine's death was only an anticipation. 'There is no lonelier man in death, except the suicide, than that man who has lived many years with a good wife and then outlived her. If two people love each other there can be no happy end to it.'

This fact, combined with the discovery of love as a reality beyond sex, gives the theme in Hemingway's work its peculiar pathos. Love brings to life its exaltation and the lack of it or destruction of it brings the unbearable loneliness that marks man's condition. All those who have really experienced love are marked by a quality of deadness once it has gone. This is a different state from that of the man who has never known love, who may ridicule it but is really speaking out of his inexperience. Robert Jordan's discovery of love was like the end of a long pilgrimage. It filled the gap which is felt but the filling of which is usually a mystery. Like the young girl wanting something but not knowing what it was. Jordan sums up:

Don't ever kid yourself about loving someone. It is just that most people are not lucky enough to have it. You never had it before and now you have it. What you have with Maria, whether it lasts just through today and a part of tomorrow, or whether it lasts for a long life is the most important thing that can happen to a human being. There will always be people who say it does not exist because they cannot have it. But I tell you it is true and that you have it and that you are lucky even if you die tomorrow.

He also has a mystical faith that love is never really destroyed. If one of the partners dies then, of course, without any sense of hereafter, the love stops. But the past love is not dead, it is still lodged in the personality. The great happiness that spreads through you after loving is never entirely dispersed. If the woman dies then the man will mourn her but the love he has known will still be part of him, more than a memory, something actually woven into his spirit. Even if she leaves you for another, the same is true because it has become part of you and cannot be taken away. He states this doctrine explicitly in *Green Hills of Africa.*

CHAPTER XV

THE WOMEN

THE most celebrated of all Hemingway's women is Lady Brett Ashley. She is a convenient symbol of the expatriate woman of the 'twenties, with no purpose in her life, and attempting to fill the void with drink and sex. The treatment she has received from the critics is also symbolic of the hasty and superficial approach to his work that has been general over the past two decades and a reminder of the need for re-assessment. Now we have had a chance to assimilate the more sensational aspects of Hemingway's genius it should be possible to probe a little more deeply into the society he portrays and its most typical representatives.

The Brett we know from hearsay, from the impressions of other writers and columnists, is not Hemingway's Brett but a legendary figure that has emerged out of simplification and faulty memory. The critic who is doing his job properly has read his source-books fairly recently, say within the last six months, and his impressions are reasonably fresh and accurate. But the reviewer or literary columnist, who deals with a dozen books a week and frequently refers to others which cling often fortuitously to his memory, may not have read anything by the writer he is discussing (save his latest work) for many years. The anatomy of significance varies widely. A person who reads *For Whom the Bell Tolls* today, especially if for the first time, will have quite a different impression of it from the person who read it when it appeared in 1940 and has not opened it since. What is more, the emphasis which a reader brings to a book from his own bias will be different and can also change in the same person over the years. Hemingway himself has said, 'The memory is never true'. Memory is apt to tell us that Brett is simply a woman who has slept too easily with too many men and lost all normal feeling and self-respect. The legend is as unlike the original as the popular idea of Mr. Micawber, created by people who have never read *David Copperfield* since childhood, is unlike Dickens' Micawber.

Theodore Bardacke, in an essay on 'Hemingway's Women', has given the conventional portrait faithfully. As far as it goes it is a truthful one, but it is still only a profile. The other side of her character is hidden from us.

> She has been emotionally stunted by a shallow world without spiritual meaning, and has become a woman devoid of womanhood. She has experienced two loveless marriages; the first with a man who died of dysentery during the war, and the second with an officer in the British Navy who returned from the war suffering from shock. Her love life, a kind of war casualty in itself, has decayed into alcoholism and a series of casual sex relations. She is 'engaged to marry' Mike who is bankrupt economically and spiritually. The sexual level of their relationship is indicated by the hotel-brothel where they stay in Paris.[1]

I want to make it clear that I am not attacking

[1] From *Ernest Hemingway: the Man and his Work*, ed. J. McCaffery.

Bardacke, who is a good critic and was primarily interested in this particular approach of Brett Ashley and her generation. But by itself it suggests that Brett is an utterly hard, insensitive and irredeemable woman. Such a view arises easily by a process of abstraction. All murderers are on the same spiritual level if you divorce them from their circumstances. Bardacke does not suggest why Brett is 'emotionally stunted' by reference to her unfortunate marriages. We must also remember that these marriages took place against a background of aimlessness and destructiveness. It is in fact the truly sensitive person who suffers most in such circumstances. A person of limited sensibility may be untouched but others will either become neurotic or, by an act of will, stubborn against fate. It is impossible to read *Fiesta* bearing this in mind, and miss Brett's honesty, awareness and sincerity. The many insincerities with which a friendly critic could charge her are obviously her little jokes and are accepted as such by her companions. That her emotions were not really stunted, but simply repressed, is clear from the scene with Jake in the taxi, when for a moment she opens the gates and confesses that in this particular situation, when her emotions are dictating to her, she has come up against another kind of barrier. To Jake she is 'a good girl wrecked by frustration'. Henry Seidel Canby calls her 'a good girl who has lost her controls'.[1] The truth is that she has reassembled her controls. There is no doubt of her frustration and we know

[1] Introduction to Modern Library Edition of *The Sun Also Rises*.

the events that led to it. But the effect on Brett was a loosening of moral conduct and a tightening of emotional control. This could be called a kind of spiritual surgery. The result is by no means satisfactory and at times is even unpleasant, but there could have been a worse fate for Lady Ashley.

According to Edmund Wilson, one of Hemingway's main characteristics is antagonism to women. He lists a number of instances in which the man behaves brutally or inconsiderately to the woman ('the instinct to get the woman down'[1] is his phrase, which is cunning because we all know such an instinct exists, but not all of us would agree to its use as a universal metaphor of the spiritual truth.) Even Jake is avenging his sex on women by being unable to give Brett what she wants. Although Wilson notes that the women in 'Macomber' and 'Kilimanjaro' are 'American bitches of the most soul-destroying sort', he fails to look further. For he is actually on the edge of an important discovery, but withdraws too quickly to make it. In all the examples he gives of this attitude, with one exception, the women are American. The one exception is the peasant's wife in 'An Alpine Idyll', which I have already referred to as an example of the crude, unsensational kind of love which exists among people who live hard, inarticulate lives.

It may be objected that Hemingway, being an American author, naturally finds the objects of his dislike among his fellow-countrymen. But most of his fiction is set outside America and there are many Europeans among his women. And he himself has

[1] *The Wound and the Bow.*

told us without qualification that American women are the hardest in the world. It is true, he put this thought into the mind of an Englishman but it was an Englishman with whom he appeared to have a great deal of sympathy.

> They are, he thought, the hardest in the world; the hardest, the cruellest, the most predatory and the most attractive and their men have softened or gone to pieces nervously as they have hardened.

And later:

> She is away for twenty minutes and now she is back, simply enamelled in that American female cruelty. They are the damnedest women. Really the damnedest.[1]

This is presumably Hemingway's contribution to the evidence of the new American matriarchy, which so delights European males, smarting under the effects of American efficiency and drive.

This is by no means an isolated instance of this attitude. Throughout his work there runs a strong current of hatred for the American female, expressed through scorn, denunciation and accusation. It comes to a head in *The Fifth Column*, when Philip flaunts a Moorish tart in the face of Dorothy, who would like to manage him. He seems to accuse American women of treating love like a business, where all the prospectuses are written by female directors and company promoters. The Moorish girl, Anita, says, 'Put the paint in the body, instead of blood. What

[1] 'The Short Happy Life of Francis Macomber'.

you get? American woman'. Here is Philip describing the background of a certain type of well-to-do American girl.

> They're all the same. Camps, colleges, money in family, now more or less than it was, usually less now, men, affairs, abortions, ambitions, and finally marry and settle down or don't marry and settle down. They open shops or work in shops, some write, others play instruments, some go on the stage, others into films. They have something called the Junior League I believe that the virgins work at. All for the public good.

A sterile career with neither peaks nor valleys, with ambition the only powerful stimulus. Philip asks Dorothy, '*Is* it true that the first thing an American woman does is to try to get the man she's interested in give up something? You know, boozing about, or smoking Virginia cigarettes, or wearing gaiters, or hunting, or something silly?'

Nothing like this and nothing comparable was ever said about English Brett, Scottish Catherine, Spanish Maria or Italian Renata. The only American woman who comes off well is Harry Morgan's wife, and she has been to neither college nor camp nor set up shop nor been in the Junior League. It is impossible to feel that Hemingway regards the moral shortcomings of Lady Ashley as anything like so destroying as the sterile aggressiveness of the American female. Ultimately the American woman seeks power over the male – not the power of love with its willing and fruitful submission but the conquest of personality demanded by the politician and business man. To compel the men to give something up, to surrender a portion of his ego, is the sign she seeks for.

The conventional love relationship is almost
impossible with such women. Man is forced to make
use of new weapons for his own defence. Where his
own sincerity might be regarded as weakness he must
repress it and replace it with less attractive qualities
which, however, will strengthen his position. The
only possible relationship is based on deceit. When
you cannot love you pretend to love. Modern 'love'
is in many cases a gigantic sham, a second-best in
default of what has been idealised but is no longer
possible. Hemingway blames the woman. In her
quest for power she has lost her earlier virtues, perhaps even the much prided 'feminine intuition'. It
is easier to cheat her than it used to be. In fact, the
truth is often lost to her, she responds best to lies
because her purposes are based on falsity. The writer
in 'Kilimanjaro' found that 'his lies were more successful with women than when he had told them the
truth'. And, dying, he made the astounding discovery
that he could actually give her more when he lied
than when he loved.

Perhaps a man steers more easily through the
reefs than a woman. Perhaps the masculine privileges
education, ballot, social freedom, loose language,
really are more easily assimilated and managed by
men than by women. It is against the spirit of the
time to deny these things to women and a modern
writer has to accept them even when he notices the
maladjustment. It is possible that the feminist vic-
tories have resulted in a psychic upheaval which has
created a new woman. This is trite in the bare state-

ment but not in its implications. For one of the major implications is that men who have been accustomed to coming to terms with one type of woman may be utterly baffled when faced with another type. There is fairly strong evidence that, despite his early sympathy if not admiration for Lady Brett, Hemingway later renounced this attitude and found the fullest literary satisfaction in the womanly woman. Catherine Barkley is not a 'new' woman. She is sufficiently pre-Shavian to say to Frederick, 'I want what you want. There isn't me any more. Just what you want.' Mrs. Morgan, Maria and Renata are all in the same old-fashioned tradition.

It is simply that Hemingway prefers the man to overpower the woman, and not vice versa. Or if 'prefer' is too positive a word, let us say that he finds the happy love affair issues out of male dominance. His predilection for 'natural man' is all of a piece with this view of the sex relationship. As has been widely noticed, there is a strong element of primitivism in this very modern writer, but the prevalence of Congolese rhythm in modern music and West African motifs in modern art should prepare us for this partnership. In *Green Hills of Africa* there is a vivid description of the hunting expedition's entry into a Masai village, and the immense impression made on the villagers by the sound of the klaxon. 'I watched the look of utter rapture and ecstasy on the women's faces and knew that with that klaxon he could have had any woman in the tribe.' We infer that this is as it should be. Kaman, the driver, could conquer not by any logical show of desirability but merely through the image of irresistible power, the klaxon.

Modern women are no longer prepared to surrender unconditionally to male power. That is the truth about the contemporary sex relationship. *Because* of this, Hemingway's implicit argument seems to run, it is no longer possible for men and women to work out a satisfactory relationship. Whether the women like it or not, submission is the basis of love. And even friendship, usually supposed to be a preparatory state, can only exist on the basis of love. 'Women made such swell friends. Awfully swell. In the first place, you had to be in love with a woman to have a basis of friendship.'[1] In other words, apart from positive dislike or indifference, the relation between men and women must be founded on male superiority. And although this view can be most easily traced in the novels subsequent to *Fiesta* it may be that part of Brett's disaster lay in her refusal to accept it. The equality of love is in fact specious, an agreement overtly to ignore the essential inequality.

So the younger women, the ones who might be expected to seek love and probably feel an impulsion towards it, find little but frustration. The causes are too obscure for them to understand why and in any case their most cherished conceptions clash with the remedy. The old consolations, especially the religious ones, have disappeared. They are lost and bewildered and cling all the more desperately to those very beliefs that are chiefly instrumental in causing the frustra-

[1] *Fiesta.*

tion. Their mothers have sometimes retained their
religious beliefs, or the shadows cast by them on conduct, and are worried and equally bewildered but at
the same time resigned because they have a simple
explanation of their dilemma. They take refuge in a
simple reversal of what seems the truth to Hemingway – man's aggressiveness is regarded as his weakness. Krebs' mother tells him she knows how weak
men are and how easily they are tempted, so she prays
for him.[1] The doctor's wife tells him that 'he who
ruleth his spirit is greater than he that taketh a city'.[2]
She is all patience and forgiveness. These are the
qualities that seem to be essential for the satisfactory
relationship: submission, acceptance, patience, forgiveness and a retreat into prayer. The young women
no longer possess them.

Few people among the younger generation will
accept this diagnosis. Catherine Barkley is no longer
true and was not even true at the time, many people
said. Both Maria and Renata are in opposition to
the popular conception of young womanhood. But
John O'Hara has a warning. It is easy to disbelieve
in these women, as he once disbelieved in Catherine
and now disbelieves in Renata, but they 'have a way
of catching up with you after you have passed them
by'.[3] It may be that Hemingway foresees the next
phase in feminist evolution and that his willing
women are forerunners.

---

[1] 'Soldier's Home', from *In Our Time.*
[2] 'The Doctor and the Doctor's Wife', *ibid.*
[3] *The New York Times Book Review*, 10 Sept. 1950.

CHAPTER XVI

THE OLD MAN AND THE SEA

THIS book was already set up in print when I received a copy of Hemingway's most recent work, *The Old Man and the Sea*. It turned out to be a small masterpiece.

It is too short to be called a novel and it is too long to be called a short story, but in technique it belongs to the latter genre. It is a very straightforward tale without sub-plots and only one sub-theme of an old fisherman who sailed too far in pursuit of a giant marlin, caught it and then lost it to sharks except for its spine and tail on the way back. Identification with the old man is so skilful and complete the story induces the tragic feeling.

It is a wonderful thing that Hemingway should have produced a work of such freshness at such a late stage in his career. It is a superb reply to those critics who believed that his genius had been eroded by analysis and complication since he planned and wrote *For Whom the Bell Tolls*.

In places this tale is a revival of the absorption in nature that gave us 'Big Two-Hearted River'. The old fisherman is engaged in an unceasing struggle with natural forces but he realises that nature is his mother and all her creatures are his brothers. His life is not really conflict; it is discipline.

Apart from its literary excellence the importance of this book lies in its truthful development from what has gone before. However often Hemingway's active, enquiring mind takes him off his natural track he always returns to it. The old animalism is still here but it has been tamed. The new lesson that Hemingway has learnt (he has a great and enviable capacity for learning) is that the secret of life lies in communion.

The old *aficionado* peeps out when we read that the marlin 'took the bait like a male and he pulls like a male'. Hemingway has not forgotten the *cojones*. But now he is accepting *cojones* as a fact, not as a triumph. The great male fish is conquered by an old man who has much of the weakness of an old man. But he is humble. He does not deify himself on account of his victory. 'Fish', he said, 'I'll stay with you until I am dead'. And 'Fish', he said, 'I love you and respect you very much. But I will kill you dead before this day ends'.

Alone on the ocean, hungry and in pain, the old man becomes a little mystical although he calls it unclear in the head. He knows that the only real thing in life is communion, the only warm and comforting thing. He knew communion with the boy who helped him but he learnt that the only everlasting communion is to be found in death. Frederick Henry had struggled towards this point of view a long time ago. The old man thinks, 'If you love him it is not a sin to kill him'. To kill is to institute an unforgettable and irreversible relationship.

I think we can look on this little book as Hemingway's *Essay on Human Understanding*. The age of all Hemingway's heroes matches his own at the time of writing. We have now gone in a straight line (except for Frederick Henry and Jake Barnes) from the Nick of the short stories to this Old Man. So many of these heroes have been hunters or at least men pitted against animals – Belmonte and Hemingway in Africa and the white hunter Wilson and now the Old Man. Man and beast are contrasted as intelligence and nobility. 'But, thank God, they are not as intelligent as we who kill them; although they are more noble and more able'. 'Man is not much beside the great birds and beasts'.

What distinguishes man, apart from his intelligence? The capacity for hope, probably. 'But man is not made for defeat. A man can be destroyed but not defeated'. 'It is silly not to hope, he thought. Besides I believe it is a sin'. Hope is a duty of man. Without it his intelligence would merely be balanced by the beast's courage and strength, and he would suffer defeat as frequently as he achieved victory. He must regard the capacity for hope as one of his most precious possessions. But he must not be arrogant or unchivalrous. He himself is a part of nature and must never drag his anchors.

This gentleness and understanding has been latent in all Hemingway's earlier work, even the most ferocious and apparently amoral. The Old Man owes a lot to bullfighters and game hunters, men whose relationship with animals has been one of frank hostility. But admiration for the bull and the lion has softened the hostility and finally produced this love of the fisherman for the marlin. Turning aside to fight Fascists and smuggle Cuban revolutionaries has not affected this steady development.

The Champion and the Defender of the Working People are not entirely absent. The Old Man dreams for a little of the time, many years ago, when he had defeated a negro in Casablanca at the hand game. He had been called The Champion after that. It's consoling to think you excel at something, even if it's only the hand game. And on the last page we are reminded of the tourists in *To Have and Have Not* – a three-line gibe against people who don't belong, who never get their facts quite right because they've missed all the early training. Hemingway's tourists are like bunting on the waterfront.

CHAPTER XVII

CODA

Hᴇᴍɪɴɢᴡᴀʏ is a writer who feels the movement of myth in his unconscious but refuses to
dilute or 'explain' contemporaneity.

The major characteristic of this contemporaneity is
its admiration for force. Culture is being
proletarianised, spiritual refinement is being
reformed.

A proletarianised culture demands a proletarianised
literature for its expression. Emphasis is on the
thing rather than its interpretation.

Hemingway's contact with the true proletariat has
been small. He knows them through their out-
posts and outlaws.

At the same time he has studied the detritus of the
old culture, those who have surrendered to the
new spirit while retaining fragments of the old.

This admiration of force is not perverted. It is a
regression. Human development oscillates between natural and political man.

Where does this bring us?

Hemingway shows us the emptiness of the Waste
Land in his own terms. Frequently he appears
to condone it and even voluntarily enter into it.
This should not concern us unless we are
moralists.

The chief contribution of his work to our understanding of this society is its emphasis on the
part played by fear in aggravating the condition;

its feeding on itself; its possible conquest by shock; or by discipline.

In his latest phase he stresses the importance of communion even if its only complete realisation lies in death. Like many other realists, Hemingway becomes a mystic against his will and judgment.

BIBLIOGRAPHY

The following books by Hemingway have been published:

1923 Three Stories and Ten Poems (Limited edition)
1924 In Our Time
1926 The Torrents of Spring
1926 Today is Friday (Limited edition)
1926 Fiesta (titled The Sun Also Rises in U.S.A.)
1927 Men Without Women
1929 A Farewell to Arms
1932 Death in the Afternoon
1933 God Rest You Merry Gentlemen (Limited edition)
1933 Winner Take Nothing
1935 Green Hills of Africa
1937 To Have and Have Not
1938 The Spanish Earth
1938 The Fifth Column and the First Forty-Nine Stories (including previous story collections)
1940 For Whom the Bell Tolls
1942 Men at War (edited by Hemingway)
1950 Across the River and Into the Trees
1952 The Old Man and the Sea

I have only been able to trace one book on Hemingway. This is *Ernest Hemingway: the Man and his Work*, edited by John K. M. McCaffery and containing essays by twenty-one writers, including the editor's introduction, on his life and work, chiefly the latter. There is interesting criticism although on the whole it gives the impression, as does most modern American criticism, of having been written by Olympians in bow ties. There is a certain humanity in the contributions by Max Eastman and Edmund Wilson and a considerable amount in John Peale Bishop's. One feels they have occasionally taken a stroll outside the college walls.

Malcolm Cowley is said to have written a valuable introduction to *The Portable Hemingway* but I have not been able to read it as British and Sudanese authors are not allowed to buy books from America.

Views on Hemingway have been expressed in notices of his books and Profiles such as Lillian Ross' in *The New Yorker* and Sam Boal's in *Park East*. These are usually fairly recent and take sides over the legend: puncture it (Ross) or inflate it (Boal).

Finally, any article on 'The Modern Novel' is compelled to notice Hemingway. The early ones were the fairest. Recent ones are subject to the same magnetic and repulsive influences as are the profile. Dependable assessments of Hemingway's work ceased to appear by about 1940. On the whole, critics are annoyed with him for developing so that their carefully stitched essays of a few years ago are now out of date and cannot be reprinted.

HEMINGWAY ON THE ENGLISH

As most of the people who read this book will be English I am including this appendix as a literary curiosity. But its genesis lies in something deeper than mere curiosity. It lies in a terrain of feeling that is of first importance to our century, when American imperialism is acting as the residual legatee of British imperialism.[1] The relationship between British and American is a matter of more than political significance. Within it lies the no-man's-land between one culture and another.

When I first read Hemingway, as a very young man, I sensed his vitality and his brutality more keenly than anything else. I was keenly aware of the fact that the Americans were the heirs to our culture and that by their drive and lack of sentimentality in matters of money and power they were creating something quite unlike what we had known before. I was especially aware of this difference of psychic atmosphere because I was brought up in a country district where I only knew two types of person: the labourers, who were dull and slow-witted, and the gentry, who were ridiculous. What chance, I used to wonder, had these people against the ruthless, hustling Americans? How the Americans must despise us for our softness

---

[1] I don't like this word imperialism in this context now. In 1952 it seemed right, but the development has been to something different, despite the Left-wing, anti-American press (1962).

and the dull evenness of our lives. I even felt a tinge of poetry in the American attitude to life, something flamboyant and courageous and Elizabethan.

Hemingway stood for The American in my mental picture of this antithesis. At the same time as I enjoyed reading him there was a shudder at the back of my mind for the inevitable contempt that he was bound to feel for anything English. A man who wrote of such an irresponsible society as the American expatriates' must regard our settled social system with its mossy tradition as a strangely preserved fossil. The slowness and prosiness of our speech must irritate him beyond words. And the importance of marriage must strike him as a detestable survival. I was, I repeat, very young and very innocent.

But I was only innocent of Hemingway. The attitude I have outlined does exist and can be seen in the works of other American writers, who refer to British royalty and aristocracy with a democratic sneer and to the security of our society with the contempt one reserves for milksops and stay-at-homes. In recent years this attitude has been weakened because the English are becoming Americanised and titled business men can be as harsh and corrupt as American *parvenus*. But in general, and in particular among the masses, who always lag a generation or so behind actuality, the attitude I have described still exists. In brief, it is a vision of the British as a race of bewildered dodos.

The great discovery was that Hemingway did not share this attitude. This very modern writer did not castigate the English for their lack of modernity.

He even seemed to think they were 'all right'. And having attempted to show how untrue the popular view of Hemingway's literary personality is in various fields, I think there is considerable consistency in this further, if minor, discovery. Just as he did not relish the collapse of standards but rather saw the void it had left, just as he did not regard sex as a satisfactory substitute for love, so he did not share the opinion that painless extermination was the best fate for a race of anachronistic Victorians.

In his first stories he appeared to have an ambivalent attitude towards the English, a combination of love and hate, probably the early adolescent contempt which a young American was liable to feel, giving way to a puzzled admiration. It is not really possible to state whether his frequent use of English idiom comes from mockery or appreciation. 'It was a frightfully hot day ... It was absolutely topping ... We were frightfully put out ...' This is from a description of taking pot-shots at the enemy as they climb over a barricade on a bridge. They are certainly not natural words for Hemingway to use. They are English to the core and one of them, 'topping', is dead and buried. It could be poking fun. But it could also be a sincere adaption of the language of English sporting circles.

By the time *Fiesta* was being written Hemingway had definitely succumbed to the attractions of this language and the state of mind that produces it. One of the most delightful characters in this book is the English tourist Harris. He may not be 'effective' or 'efficient' but he is fresh, friendly and sincere. His

language, of course, is not fresh for the English well-
to-do have reduced language to a cipher, but its very
monotony gives a sensation of something struggling
to escape. 'I say, I do, you know ... Be a good
chap'. Jake liked Harris and so did Hemingway. He
uses this language with relish but never mocks it.

In the same book he states how easy it is, being
with English, to get into the habit of using English
expression in your thinking. This expression is admirably adapted to the sporting life and the avoidance
of emotion. 'The English spoken language – the
upper classes, anyway – must have fewer words than
the Eskimo ..... The English talked with inflected
phrases. One phrase to mean everything. I liked them,
though. I liked the way they talked. Take Harris.'
It is already quite plain how far Hemingway has
moved from the robust American attitude towards
the effete English. At that time British films could
not be shown on American screens, partly because of
the accent which was considered unbearable.

Another American convention is that the English are stand-offish. Their tourists used to be worth
a laugh anywhere. (I once travelled in Germany with
an Englishman who wouldn't eat breakfast if he
couldn't have bacon and eggs.) A group of twenty-
five Englishwomen sat in a car and watched the fiesta
through their glasses. A solid phalanx of *noli me
tangere*. And yet Hemingway's personal opinion is
that you only find true friendship, the kind that
accepts without conditions, among the best of the
English, the best of the Hungarians and the very best
Spaniards: 'the thing that used to be the most clear

distinction of nobility when there was nobility'
(*Green Hills of Africa*).

During Hemingway's 'Death' phase the English
again came out well. It was not that they are interested in death, as Hemingway was, but the exact
reverse; they ignore death and concentrate on life.
It was the categorical aspect of this attitude that
attracted Hemingway. Be interested in death because
it comes to all of us and we have the power to give
it. Be interested in life because we are in it. It is
the merging of the two, in the teutonic fashion, that
he dislikes. Here is the relevant passage.

> The English and the French live for life... The
> English live for this world and death is not a thing to
> think of, to consider, to mention, to seek, or to risk
> except in the service of the country, or for sport, or for
> adequate reward. Otherwise it is an unpleasant subject
> to be avoided, or at best, moralised on, but never to be
> studied. Never discuss casualties, they say, and I have
> heard them say it very well. When the English kill
> they kill for sport... (*Death in the Afternoon.*)

And so it came as a bitter blow when the Colonel
in *Across the River* said the British 'could not fight
their way out of a wet tissue towel'. Reading the
critics, one was led to believe that this statement was
the message of the whole book. Few people seemed to
consider that that was just what a somewhat bigoted
and tired American might say and did say. They did
not realise that Montgomery's reputation, based on
overwhelming armour, might irritate many fighting
men (American as well as British). Even American
critics, the kind who believe the main function of a

novel is to make the contemporary political set-up look attractive, were appalled. A writer doesn't trouble to answer this kind of thing in public but he still thinks in private. And, in this particular case, this is what he says in a letter.

> Because I gave my American Colonel the usual American prejudices of his trade it was considered an attack on Field Marshal Bernard Law Montgomery and British valour etc. I hope to God I have seen enough of British valor (spell it either way) and non valor in my life to not constitute myself a critic.